Getting the most from Windows XP

Jim Gatenby

BERNARD BABANI (publishing) LTD
The Grampians
Shepherds Bush Road
London W6 7NF
England

www.babanibooks.com

Please Note

Although every care has been taken with the production of this book to ensure that any projects, designs, modifications and/or programs, etc., contained herewith, operate in a correct and safe manner and also that any components specified are normally available in Great Britain, the Publishers and Author do not accept responsibility in any way for the failure (including fault in design) of any project, design, modification or program to work correctly or to cause damage to any equipment that it may be connected to or used in conjunction with, or in respect of any other damage or injury that may be so caused, nor do the Publishers accept responsibility in any way for the failure to obtain specified components.

Notice is also given that if equipment that is still under warranty is modified in any way or used or connected with home-built equipment then that warranty may be void.

First published - April 2002
Reprinted - September 2002
Reprinted - August 2003

British Library Cataloguing in Publication Data:

A catalogue record for this book is available from the
British Library

ISBN 0 85934 515 7
Cover Design by Gregor Arthur
Printed and bound in Great Britain by Cox and Wyman Ltd

About this Book

Windows XP unites the Windows 98 operating system, popular with home users, with the ultra reliable Windows NT/Windows 2000 systems predominant in business. Windows XP has a brand new "look and feel", with a simplified *start* menu and a clear *Desktop*. *Task Panes* on the left of the screen give instant access to frequently-used activities.

This book builds on the author's earlier titles, such as "Windows 98 hard disc and file management", and embraces the many powerful new features built into Windows XP. These include the *Windows Media Player*, *Network Setup Wizard*, *Internet Connection Sharing*, *Internet Connection Firewall*, *CD-burning*, *System Restore* and *Compressed Folders*. The new Windows Media Player is packed with features to enhance the playing and management of audio and video files, including those downloaded from the Internet.

Windows XP includes its own CD-burning software which integrates seamlessly into the Windows interface. This allows users to create their own music CDs and to easily back up important files onto this high capacity storage medium, which is both cheap and very durable.

This book is aimed at the new Windows XP user, who wishes to manage their computer efficiently, while making the most of the powerful features introduced in Windows XP. The book starts by describing the saving of your work in an organized set of personal folders instead of haphazard, unstructured saving destinations.

To keep the computer running in peak condition, Windows XP provides a number of maintenance tools. These include *Error-checking*, *Disk Cleanup* and *Disk Defragmenter*, which should be used regularly. These tools are described, together with *System Restore*, a new feature which returns a faulty computer to an earlier healthy configuration. Disaster often strikes in the form of *viruses* and accidental deletion of data. The book describes how peace of mind can be achieved with the use of third party *anti-virus software* and sensible *backup procedures*, including backups to *CD-R* and *CD-RW* using the software built into Windows XP.

Windows XP has many features to support *networking*, from the smallest two-computer home network up to the worldwide Internet. These features are discussed in simple language, including setting up the hardware and software and then starting to use them. Connecting computers to form a network is very cost-effective in terms of shared resources. The *Network Setup Wizard* introduced with Windows XP makes this a much easier task and shields the user from the most obscure jargon and technicalities. All you need is an inexpensive network card for each machine and cable(s) to connect them. *Wireless technology*, which allows you to network your home without laying a single cable or drilling holes in walls, etc., is also discussed.

The Internet Connection Sharing feature in Windows XP enables several computers on a home or small business network to share a single Internet connection using one modem and a telephone line. The new *Internet Connection Firewall* prevents your computers from being attacked and damaged from outside by "hackers" using the Internet.

Later chapters cover the above networking topics before describing the method of *fitting a new modem* to your computer. Also discussed are faster and more expensive methods of connection such as *ISDN*, *ADSL* and *Cable Modems*. Points to consider when choosing an *Internet Service Provider* are listed, followed by a step-by-step description of the process of getting on-line to the Internet.

Outlook Express, the e-mail program in Windows XP, is described including the sending and receiving of e-mail *attachments* such as the exchange of *photographs* between friends and family, for example.

The final chapter describes the Windows Media Player and its many features for managing and playing audio and video files. Use of such software will surely increase in the future when cheaper and more readily-available *broadband* Internet connections allow much faster downloading and *streaming* of audio files and *video on demand*. Also covered are other features of the Windows Media Player such as the *Internet Radio Tuner* and the copying of CDs to a hard disc to create your own *Media Library* and *Playlists*. *Burning* your own *audio CDs* by copying files from your hard disc using Windows XP is also described.

About the Author

Jim Gatenby trained as a Chartered Mechanical Engineer and initially worked at Rolls-Royce Ltd using computers in the analysis of performance. He obtained a Master of Philosophy degree in Mathematical Education by research at Loughborough University of Technology and taught mathematics and computing to 'A' Level for many years. His most recent posts have included Head of Computer Studies and Information Technology Coordinator. During this time he has written many books in the fields of educational computing and Microsoft Windows.

The author has considerable experience of teaching students of all ages and abilities, in school and in adult education. For several years he successfully taught the well-established CLAIT course (Computer Literacy and Information Technology) from Oxford Cambridge and RSA Examinations, as well as GCSE and National Curriculum Information Technology courses.

Trademarks

Contents

3

Hard Disc Care 51

4

Backup Activities 69

Introducing Windows XP

What is Windows XP?

Windows XP is a collection of software forming a computer *operating
system*. Microsoft Windows in various versions has been the dominant
operating system on personal computers for many years.

The operating system provides the environment in which we control and
interact with the computer. It presents the menus from which we select
commands or tasks, it controls the screen display and allows us to
manage our document files and folders and to save and print our work.
The operating system also controls peripheral devices such as scanners
and modems and our connection to the Internet. No matter what we use
our computer for - word processing, surfing the net, graphic design,
accountancy, composing music, video editing, etc. - the operating
system will be working in the background in overall control of the
computer.

Apart from this basic role of managing the computer and providing
various tools for routine maintenance tasks like deleting files, Windows
XP also includes *applications* software such as a Web browser, text
editors and a digital media player for working with music and video.

The Evolution of Microsoft Windows XP

Windows XP is the latest in a family of Microsoft Windows operating systems. Microsoft first started to dominate the personal computer world in 1981 with a text-only operating system called MSDOS - Microsoft Disc Operating System, often referred to as DOS. This required the user to type in rather obscure commands, in order to control the computer. For example, **AUTOEXEC.BAT**, an important file used in the computer's start up process, could be viewed and edited by typing in:

EDIT AUTOEXEC.BAT

This system required the user of MS-DOS to learn quite a lengthy list of commands - a small language in itself. Although the MS-DOS system was easily mastered by computing specialists and enthusiasts, it was difficult for the general user or the busy office worker who simply wanted to use the computer as a tool for their particular work. Companies such as Apple tackled this problem by introducing the more "user-friendly"

WIMP system, in which the computer is controlled with a mouse and a series of windows, icons and pull-down menus. This freed the user from the need to learn and type in complex operating system commands. For example, in order to print

your work using the new WIMP system you simply move the mouse pointer over the icon (or small picture) representing a printer and click the left-hand button.

Microsoft soon introduced Windows, its own version of the "Graphical User Interface". Although there were earlier versions, Windows 3.1, introduced in 1992, was the most successful of the first generation of Windows operating systems. In essence, Windows 3.1 was really just a graphical "front end", allowing the computer to be controlled with a mouse, shielding the user from the technicalities of MS-DOS, which was still running at the heart of the system.

Windows 95 and 98 and Me subsequently appeared, introducing many new features, but still based on the original MS-DOS foundation.

However, business users were provided with their own versions of Windows, namely Windows NT followed by Windows 2000. These were based on a completely new design, no longer using the old MS-DOS system as a foundation.

Windows 95, 98 and Me were primarily aimed at the home user, and while perfectly capable of running business programs, were also very suited to other areas of computing, such as games requiring sound and high quality graphics. Windows Me in particular introduced a new media player with facilities for copying and managing music CDs and for editing home videos.

Windows NT and Windows 2000, with their emphasis on business applications, were particularly strong on networking and security. In addition, being a completely new design, not based on the old MS-DOS system, they were more stable and reliable, not susceptible to "crashing" or locking up, as some users found with Windows 98, for example.

For simplicity, it was desirable for Microsoft to merge the two Windows families (often referred to as Windows 9X and Windows NT) into a single operating system suitable for both home and business users. This would need to provide the multi-media facilities demanded by home users combined with the reliability and networking capability required in business.

Windows XP is the result of this coalition between the two Windows families. In fact, there are two versions of Windows XP, known as Windows XP Home Edition and Windows XP Professional. The two versions are basically the same, both using the proven Windows NT technology, known for its reliability and stability. The Home Edition is a sub-set of the Professional Edition, the latter having additional features for large organisation network management and security.

Windows XP Innovations and Improvements

- The screens have been redesigned and are less cluttered.

- The Windows XP computer is more reliable, unlikely to "crash" or lock up with a "frozen" mouse pointer or a "fatal error" message on a blue screen.

- The Windows XP computer starts up and runs faster than earlier versions of Windows, such as Windows 98.

- Several people can set up individual **User Accounts** on the same computer, with their own password and settings.

- Multi-media facilities have been improved with more support for digital photography, music and video editing.

- Windows XP includes greater support for networking, including home networks, wireless networking, connections between remote computers and video conferencing.

- Windows XP supports **Internet Connection Sharing**, allowing several computers, connected to a home or small office network, to use a single Internet Connection.

- Windows XP includes an **Internet Connection Firewall** to shield small home networks from unwelcome traffic from the Internet and to prevent "hackers" from invading the computer. A firewall may also be used to restrict the *outgoing* Internet traffic to approved Web sites only.

- The settings on a computer might be corrupted by a particular event (such as the installation of new hardware or software). The **System Restore** feature allows a computer to revert to a previous configuration when the computer was working properly. These earlier configurations are known as *restore points* and are like snapshots of all of the crucial settings. Restore points are recorded automatically from time to time. You can also create a restore point manually if you feel it is appropriate.

- Windows XP includes its own software for burning CD-Rs and writing to CD-RW discs.

Moving Up to Windows XP

Hardware Requirements

As the Microsoft Windows operating system has evolved over the years it has become packed with more and more sophisticated features, demanding ever more powerful computers in order to run at an acceptable speed. According to Microsoft, Windows XP requires a computer having the following *minimum* specification:

- PC with 300MHz or higher processor speed
- 64MB of RAM minimum but 128MB or higher recommended
- 1.5GB of available hard disc space
- CD-ROM or DVD drive

Please note that these are minimum figures. A machine only just meeting the specification may work slowly - some people have said that 500MHz is the minimum processor speed to give acceptable performance.

If you have a computer on which you want to run Windows XP and which does not meet these minimum specifications, it may be worth upgrading, i.e. replacing one or more of the critical components listed above. This can be very much cheaper than buying a brand new machine. There will probably be several small businesses in your area specializing in building and upgrading computers and able to undertake the work at a reasonable price.

Purchasing the Windows XP Software

If you are already running Windows 98, Windows 98 Second Edition, Windows Millenium (Me), Windows NT 4.0 or Windows 2000 Professional, you can buy an *upgrade* version of Windows XP. This is considerably cheaper than buying the full version.

There are two editions of Windows XP, called Home and Professional. Windows XP Professional contains some additional features required by large business networks, otherwise the two versions are the same.

Installing Windows XP

The installation process is started by inserting the self-booting Windows XP CD and responding to the on-screen instructions. The whole operation takes about an hour. However, since Windows XP is a new operating system you may find there are problems of compatibility with some of your old hardware and software. If you are upgrading from an existing version of Windows, such as Me, the installation may be interrupted while you are warned about compatibility issues. In some cases you may be advised to remove software and perhaps re-install afterwards. In the case of incompatible hardware, you may need to visit the manufacturer's Web site to obtain modified *driver* software (discussed shortly).

Alternatively, you can check the compatibility of your system before starting the installation by selecting **Check system compatibility** from the Windows XP CD, as shown below.

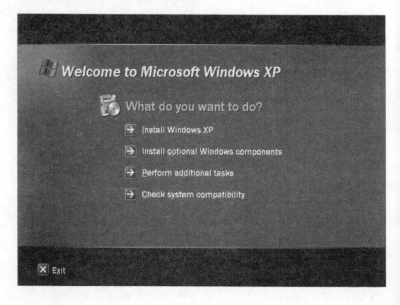

Device Drivers

Whenever we buy a new piece of hardware, it must be compatible with our particular operating system. Special programs, called *drivers*, allow the operating system to work with a particular device. If you buy a new printer or scanner, for example, driver software is usually included in the package. Windows XP itself should also include drivers to allow it to work with many of the most common devices.

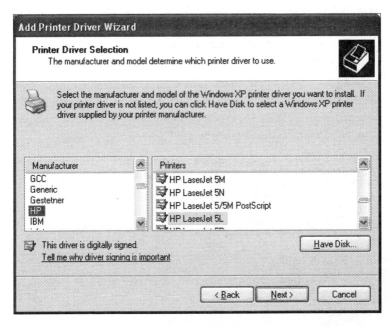

However, with a very new operating system such as Windows XP it takes time for the manufacturers of peripheral devices such as printers, modems, etc., to provide the necessary driver software. If you are using an older model of printer, for example, you may find it is no longer supported, i.e. neither Microsoft nor the printer manufacturer are providing the necessary driver software to enable the device to work with Windows XP.

After installing Windows XP on one of my computers, I found an intermittent problem with print quality which hadn't occurred before Windows XP was installed. On logging onto the Internet and checking the Microsoft Hardware Compatibility list, I found that my particular printer was not currently supported by Windows XP. This list can be viewed at:

http://www.microsoft.com/hcl

This suggested that the printer itself would need to be replaced unless I could obtain a suitable driver from another source. As stated earlier, Windows XP is a close relative of Windows 2000. A visit to the printer manufacturer's Web site showed that a Windows 2000 driver was available for my model of printer. Downloading the Windows 2000 driver and installing it in Windows XP solved my problem with the print quality.

In general, where manufacturers of peripheral devices are not yet able to supply drivers compatible with Windows XP it may be worth trying a Windows 2000 driver, if available. Driver software can usually be downloaded free from the manufacturer's Web site.

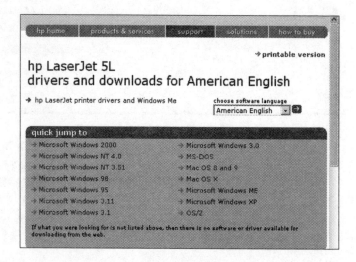

Product Activation

This is a new software feature intended to prevent, for example, a home or small business user buying one CD and installing it on several computers, a practice known as *casual copying* and regarded as theft. Product Activation is aimed at the purchaser of a single Windows XP CD - it does not apply to large organizations buying multiple copies or to new computers supplied with Windows XP already installed.

The activation process relies on a unique *installation ID*. This is a number based partly on the *product key*, the string of 25 characters supplied on your Windows XP folder which you must type in during the installation process. The remainder of the installation ID is based on information automatically derived from the hardware components in your computer. Product Activation means your copy of the Windows XP CD can only be used to install Windows XP on your particular computer.

If you wish, activation can take place in response to a prompt during the Windows XP installation process. Otherwise, if you don't activate Windows XP straightaway, you can still use the software but only for the next 30 days. During this time you will be reminded to activate the software. After 30 days, Windows XP will cease to function, apart from the activation feature. During the 30 days there is an activation icon in the system tray. The activation process can also be started by clicking:

start/All Programs/Accessories/System Tools/Activate Windows

Activation can be carried out over the Internet or by a telephone call to Microsoft. The activation process does not require any personal information.

If you make several changes to the hardware components of your computer, you may need to repeat the activation process at some point in the future. In practice, the activation process is quite straight forward and only takes a few minutes.

Product Activation is not to be confused with *registration* in which you supply details like your name and address, to ensure that you receive support and details of future Microsoft product updates.

A Brief Tour of Windows XP

The next few pages give an overview of some of the main features of Windows XP. Most of the topics are discussed in more detail in the remainder of the book. You will see that in addition to providing the software tools to run your computer, Windows XP also provides a wealth of software to maintain the system and carry out modifications. Windows XP also includes many *applications* of its own. These are programs which might otherwise be bought separately from alternative suppliers, and cover tasks such as browsing the Internet, sending e-mails, drawing and painting, editing text and working with digital media.

When you switch the computer on, you should notice that Windows XP starts up more quickly than earlier versions of Windows such as Windows 98. If the computer has been set up for several people to use, select your user name from the list of users, as shown below, and if necessary enter your password.

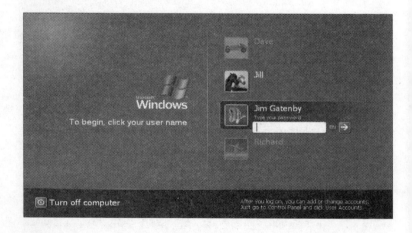

This gives you access to your own area of the computer, personalised with your preferred settings and giving secure access to your files.

The next screen to appear is the Windows Desktop, with the **start** button in the bottom left-hand corner and the Windows TaskBar along the bottom, as shown in the screenshot below. Apart from an icon for the **Recycle Bin** (discussed later), the Desktop on a new installation of Windows XP is completely clear. If you are upgrading from an earlier version of Windows, your previous Desktop icons will be retained.

It is still possible to place shortcut icons on the Windows XP Desktop to give quick access to frequently used programs and files. However, Windows XP has reduced the need for shortcut icons by automatically placing frequently used programs and recent documents in a pop-up **start Menu** which appears when you click the **start** button.

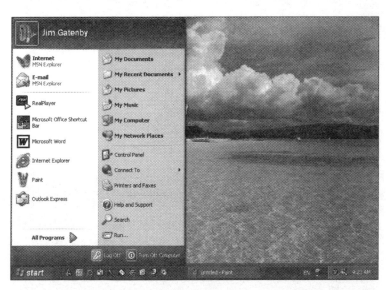

Entries can be deleted from the list of frequently used programs on the left of the panel. Entries in the list **My Recent Documents** in the right-hand panel can be deleted in a similar way. **My Documents**, **My Pictures** and **My Music**, shown previously, are folders provided by Windows XP for storing any files you create in those categories. With experience, you will probably wish to create your own folders and sub-folders, as discussed later in this book.

My Computer

Referring to the **start Menu** on the previous page, **My Computer** listed in the right-hand panel is a very important tool used in the management of Microsoft Windows. Clicking **My Computer** in the **start Menu** brings up the window shown below.

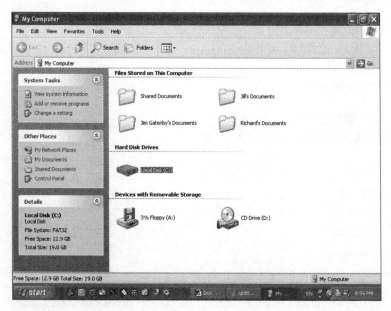

My Computer allows you to look at the various resources on your computer, such as disc drives and CDs. Amongst other things you can carry out maintenance tasks such as cleaning up your hard disc by deleting unwanted files. The panel at the bottom left of the **My Computer** window above shows statistics such as the amount of free disc space.

Both My Computer and the Windows Explorer discussed next allow you to organize and manage your work in a system of files and folders.

The Windows Explorer

The Windows Explorer lists all the resources of your computer (disc drives, folders, sub-folders, etc.,) in a hierarchy down the left-hand side of the screen, as shown below. A quick way to launch Explorer (not to be confused with Internet Explorer), is to right click the **start** button, then select **Explorer** from the pop-up menu which appears.

The right panel shows the contents of any folders you have opened. You can carry out a variety of management tasks on the folders and files listed in Explorer by right clicking over the appropriate name or icon. This produces a menu as shown above at the lower right.

Amongst other things, the menu includes options to copy, delete, rename and create a shortcut to a file or folder from the Windows XP Desktop.

Launching Programs

We have seen that frequently used programs are automatically placed on the left-hand of the **start** menu for easy access. If desired, commonly used programs and files can also be launched from *shortcut icons* on the Windows XP Desktop, as discussed elsewhere in this book. The main bulk of your programs, however, are launched by selecting **start** and **All Programs**, as shown below.

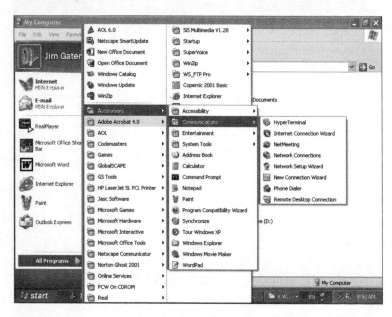

The programs listed on the **All Programs** menu shown above are a mixture of the software applications you have installed (such as your favourite word processing or painting package) together with a vast range of software applications and tools provided on the Windows XP CD. Many of Windows XP's own programs are reached from the **Accessories** menu shown above. These include the Windows **Paint** program, **Windows Explorer** (discussed shortly) and the **Notepad** and **WordPad** text processors for creating and editing simple documents.

The Windows Media Player allows you to create and manage your own music CDs and edit home movies. Menu options with a right pointing arrow lead to further menus such as the **Communications** menu off the **Accessories** menu shown previously and below. This menu contains a number of options for setting up your network and Internet connections, as shown below on the right.

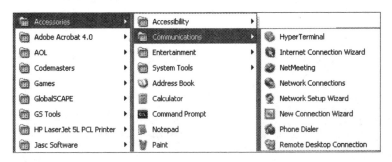

Another important feature within the **Accessories** menu is **System Tools**, shown below on the right. This menu includes a number of tools intended to keep your computer running efficiently, such as **Disk Cleanup**, **Disk Defragmenter** and **System Restore**.

Topics such as home networking and using the system tools are discussed in more detail later in this book.

The Control Panel

This is an essential component of Windows XP, used (amongst other things) for altering settings and adding and removing new hardware and software. The **Control Panel** can be launched by clicking its name in the previously shown **start menu**. Alternatively click **Change a setting** in the **System Tasks** menu on the left of **My Computer**. The Control Panel opens in the **Category view** shown below. This view shows the tasks which can be performed using the Control Panel.

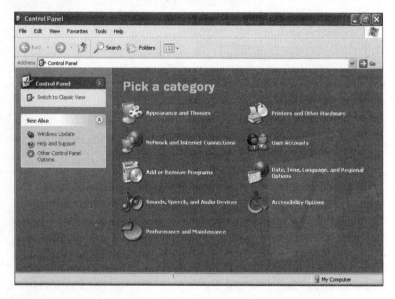

Earlier versions of Windows showed the Control Panel displaying a set of icons representing the various tools. This arrangement is still available in Windows XP and can be selected by clicking the option **Switch to Classic View** shown in the Control Panel above.

The Control Panel in Classic View is shown on the next page. Both views of the Control Panel also give access to **Windows Update**. Clicking this option connects your computer to the Internet where you are given the opportunity to download the latest versions of software relevant to your computer.

In the **Control Panel**, as shown above, changes are made to settings after double clicking the appropriate icon. For example, double clicking **Display** allows you to change all of your screen colours and to select a screen saver. Many of the tools in the Control Panel are discussed in detail later in this book.

The Recycle Bin

This is a container for your deleted files and folders. The Recycle Bin can be launched by double-clicking its icon on the Windows XP Desktop. Files and folders sent to the Recycle Bin can still be retrieved unless the bin has been emptied. Files and folders in the Recycle Bin are still taking up space on your hard disc.

Home and Small Office Networking

Many homes and small businesses now have more than one computer, and can benefit from simple networking to share resources such as disc drives, files, printers and an Internet connection. Windows XP provides the **Network Setup Wizard** to simplify the task of linking two or more computers. **My Network Places**, accessed from the **start Menu**, allows you to look at the resources on your network. For example, on my home machine consisting of two linked computers, I can use **My Network Places** to view (side by side on the same screen), the contents of the hard discs of both machines. This makes it very easy to copy files and folders between computers. Using a second computer in this way provides a very fast and convenient backup system, apart from the ability to share a single printer.

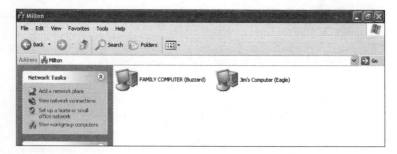

Internet Connection Sharing, a feature of Windows XP, allows two or more computers on a small network to connect to the Internet using a single modem or some other type of Internet Connection. Setting up local area networks and Internet Connection Sharing in Windows XP are made easy by the use of step-by-step wizards. So the work can be carried out by literally anyone and does not require a high degree of technical knowledge or skill.

That completes our brief tour which was intended to give an overview of some of the main components of Windows XP. These features are described in more detail in the remainder of this book.

2

Managing Files and Folders

Introduction

This section gives an overview of the way Windows XP can be used to organise your work into a hierarchy of files and folders. The term *file*, in this context, refers to a single piece of work stored on the hard disc. The piece of work may be, for example, a letter or report, a spreadsheet, a drawing or a set of records in a database.

In the same way that loose papers in the traditional office are organised into *folders*, computer files are grouped into metaphorical folders on the hard disc. This makes it easier to find a particular piece of work. Disc management tasks such as copying or deleting groups of files become much simpler. Folders are a graphical representation of the text-based *directories* used in earlier systems. Windows XP has two component programs which can be used for managing files and folders; Windows Explorer and My Computer.

The Windows Explorer

Explorer can be opened using **start**, **All Programs**, **Accessories** and **Windows Explorer**. However, a quicker method is to click the *right* mouse button over the **start** button, then select **Explore**.

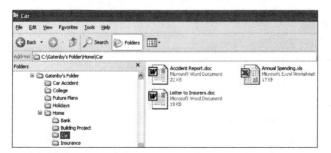

As shown on the left of the previous screenshot, Windows Explorer is particularly useful for viewing the hierarchical or branching structure of the various discs and their folders. Folders can be opened up to reveal the *subfolders* and files within.

My Computer

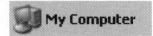

This is launched by clicking **My Computer** off the **start** menu. **My Computer** gives an immediate view of the different disc storage devices on your system.

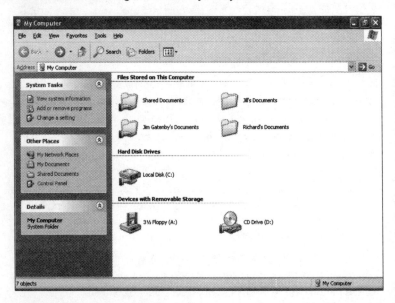

A single click on the icon for a drive highlights the drive and reveals statistics such as the total size and the amount of free space. Double-clicking on the icon for a disc drive, such as drive **C:** reveals the folders and files on the disc.

In addition to file and folder management tasks, My Computer can also give access to various features such as the **Control Panel** used in the setting up and management of the computer, the adding and removal of software and access to any available network resources through **My Network Places**.

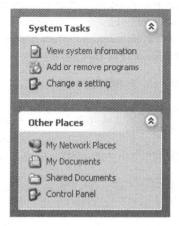

System Tasks

View system information

Add or remove programs

Change a setting

Other Places

My Network Places

My Documents

Shared Documents

Control Panel

View system information allows you to see the technical specification of your computer and make changes to hardware settings through the **System Properties** feature shown below.

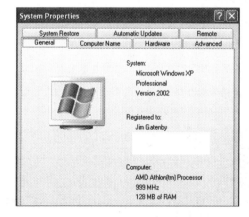

The **Device Manager**, accessed from the **Hardware** tab shown above, displays settings for the main components of your computer, allows you to check they are working correctly and make alterations if necessary.

Both the Windows Explorer and My Computer can be used for managing files and folders from the **File and Folder Tasks** panel (discussed shortly), or by "dragging" and "dropping" with the mouse or by using the menus accessed from **File** and **Edit**. These topics are covered in detail later in this chapter.

Windows Explorer and My Computer have a number of browser type features which can be switched on and off, such as the **Back** and **Forward** buttons to enable movement between windows, and an **Address** bar showing the path to the currently selected file or folder.

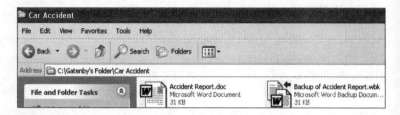

These features can be switched on and off using the **View/Toolbars** menu.

Folder Options

Windows XP provides a number of alternative ways of displaying folders in My Computer and the Windows Explorer. You can customize the folders by selecting **Tools** and **Folder Options...** from the menu bar across the top of My Computer and the Windows Explorer.

Selecting **Use Windows classic folders** will mean that the **File and Folder Tasks** menu is not displayed down the left-hand side of the window. There is an option for all folders to be opened in the same window or for each folder to open in a separate window of its own. You can also choose between single or double click mouse operations to open a folder.

The Folder "My Documents"

My Documents

Windows XP is designed to simplify the organisation of your work into folders. When Windows XP is first installed on your computer, a folder called **My Documents** is automatically provided, normally located on the **C:** drive. When you save a new piece of work, it is placed, by default, into **My Documents**. Experienced users create folders of their own with meaningful names, then select the required folder before saving their work. This makes it easier to locate and retrieve files at a later date. Creating your own folders is discussed shortly, but using **My Documents** is a good place to start when you are learning to save your work. **My Documents** is often used as the default folder when files are downloaded to your hard disc from the Internet. (The default folder is suggested automatically at the start of the downloading process although you can override this by selecting a folder of your choice).

Opening up the folder My Documents in the Windows Explorer on one of my computers, as shown below, illustrates that a folder can contain other folders (i.e. sub-folders within a folder) as well as files. In the right-hand panel below, there are several sub-folders such as **My Pictures, My Videos**, **My Webs** and **My Music** provided by Windows XP by default and allowing you to organize your files into categories.

Files are identified by their different icons and filename extensions (**.doc**, **.htm**, **.mdb**, **.gif**, etc.) and these are discussed in detail shortly.

The Hierarchy of Folders

The previous window showing the folder **My Documents** also contains folders within it, known as "subfolders".

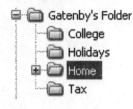

The Windows Explorer displays the branching or hierarchical structure of folders and subfolders. Shown on the left is **Gatenby's Folder** with 4 subfolders branching off. The **+** sign indicates that a folder contains more folders within it.

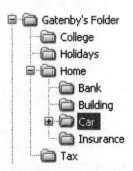

Clicking on the **+** sign against the folder **Home** reveals four subfolders, **Bank**, **Building**, **Car** and **Insurance**. (Clicking the **-** sign on the left of **Home** hides the subfolders **Bank**, **Building**, **Car** and **Insurance**).

Files and folders within the folder **Car** are revealed in the Windows Explorer right-hand panel by clicking on the folder icon. The **Size** and **Type** of file are displayed when you select **View** and **Details** from the Explorer menu.

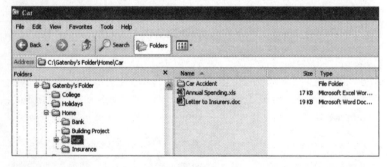

The folder **Car** shown above contains 2 files and a folder, **Car Accident**. The files are a Word document and an Excel spreadsheet. Note that Windows XP, like Windows 98 and Me before it, allows files to be saved with long filenames such as "**Letter to Insurers**".

Files in Detail

There are two main types of file on your computer: *software* and *data files*.

Software

The software used to run your computer is made up of many different *program files* designed to carry out specific tasks. The *systems software*, such as the Windows XP operating system, is used to control all of the basic functions of the computer and to provide the interface with the user. The systems software is essential no matter what purpose you intend to use the computer for.

The *applications software* (such as Microsoft Office or Internet Explorer) includes the programs you buy and install to carry out a task such as word processing, drawing or accounts work. Program files have filename extensions like **.exe** (discussed shortly).

The non-expert user should never attempt to modify or move program files, as this will almost certainly cause major problems.

Data Files

These files are the work you produce and save on the hard disc. A data file may be, for example, a word processing document, database records, spreadsheets, pictures, photographs or music. Initially you will be concerned with creating and naming new files but later you will need to perform tasks such as copying, moving, renaming and deleting files. You may also create new folders to organize your data files efficiently.

Types of Data File

When a file is created by saving in one of the applications, such as Microsoft Word, Excel or Access, for example, an icon is attached to the filename to indicate the type of file, as shown below:

 Customer list.mdb
Microsoft Access Application
332 KB

 New logo.bmp
800 x 600
Bitmap Image

 Further Advance.doc
Microsoft Word Document
22 KB

 Monthly Accounts.xls
Microsoft Excel Workshee
15 KB

Filename Extensions

Although Windows XP doesn't always display them, files are automatically saved with a 3-letter extension after the filename, which identifies the file type. For example, some program files are saved with the **.exe** extension. In the text-only MSDOS operating system which preceded the various icon-based Windows systems, files were listed in directories with filenames such as **myfile.doc** or **program.exe**. Since there were no icons in these early systems, the extension was necessary to show the type of file.

You can switch on the filename extensions in Windows XP by highlighting the required folder in Explorer or My Computer, then selecting **Tools**, **Folder Options…** and the **View** tab. To display the file extensions remove the tick in the box to the left of **Hide extensions for known file types**.

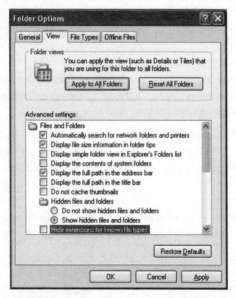

After switching on the filename extensions as described above, the full details of the files can be displayed in the Windows Explorer or My Computer, as shown on the next page.

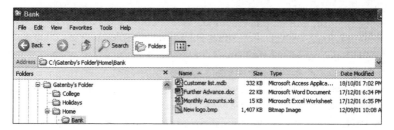

Shown above are the filename extensions **.xls**, **.doc**, **.mdb**, and **.bmp**, representing files produced in Excel, Word, Access and Paint respectively.

To display all of the information shown above you need to switch on **View** and **Details** from the Explorer (or My Computer) menu bar. You may need to stretch the columns to see all of the details, by dragging the small vertical bars, e.g. between **Name** and **Size**, etc.

The **Tools/Folder Options.../View** dialogue box shown below and on the previous page also allows you to completely hide particular types of file, such as operating system files or those with certain attributes, such as Hidden. (File attributes are discussed in the next section). The filenames of hidden files will therefore not be listed in the Windows Explorer or My Computer. This is a good idea since it makes it harder to delete important system files essential for the operation of the computer.

Switch on **Display the full path ...** in both boxes below if you want to see, for example, **C:\Gatenby's Folder\Home\Bank**, for example, rather than simply **Bank**. This option can be set for both the title bar and the address bar in Windows Explorer and My Computer, as shown below.

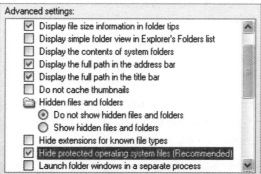

File Properties

When a file is saved, it is automatically given certain properties and attributes. The user may view and perhaps change these properties in My Computer or the Windows Explorer. To view a file's properties, highlight the filename by moving the cursor over it. The filename should be surrounded by a coloured background. Now click the *right* button; a menu appears which includes, amongst others, the option to display the file **Properties.** (You can also access **Properties** using **File** on the menu bar across the top of the Explorer or My Computer window).

Selecting **Properties** allows you to view the file details and change the file attributes if necessary.

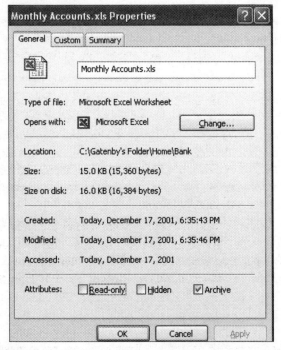

The **Properties** dialogue box above shows the icon attached to the file by Windows XP - in this case denoting an Excel worksheet i.e a file with the **.xls** extension.

File Attributes

At the bottom of the properties dialogue box are the file attributes **Read-only**, **Hidden** and **Archive**.

Switching these attributes on with a tick in the adjacent box has the following effects:

Read-Only

You can view the contents of the file but the file cannot be altered or deleted. This attribute would be switched on to protect important files which you don't want deleted (either accidentally or deliberately).

Hidden

Confidential files can be protected by switching this attribute on. Anyone else using the computer will not be aware of the existence of hidden files. The filename will not appear when you view the contents of folders using the Windows Explorer or My Computer or when you do **File** and **Open...** to reveal a list of files in an application such as Word. To open a hidden file, you need to know the filename and type it in during a **File** and **Open...** operation.

To make sure your "hidden" files really are hidden you need to tell My Computer or the Windows Explorer to hide them as discussed previously. This is done by selecting **Tools**, **Folder Options...** and the **View** tab. Then switch on the option **Do not show hidden files and folders**.

Archive

This is used by special backup programs which are set to make regular duplicate copies of important files. If the archive attribute is ticked, the file will be included in the next backup operation.

Working with Files and Folders

This section deals with the common tasks involved in organizing and maintaining your folders and the files you have produced in Word, Excel, Access, etc. These tasks include copying, moving, deleting and renaming files and folders.

Before files and folders can be examined or manipulated they must be selected or highlighted then opened with the mouse. Windows XP allows you to perform these tasks using either a single click or double click of the left-hand mouse button. This option can be set in the **Folder Options** dialogue box mentioned earlier. This is accessed by selecting **Tools, Folder Options...** and the **General** tab from the menu bar in the Windows Explorer or My Computer.

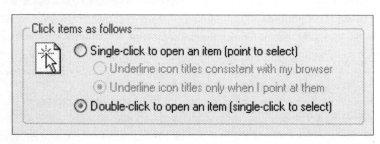

After you switch on the radio buttons of your choice as shown above, click **Apply** and **OK** for your selection to take effect. Then, depending on the option you have chosen, you will be able to use either a single or double click of the left mouse button to carry out the following operations:

- Open a folder to reveal any files or subfolders.

- Start a program running from an icon on the Windows Desktop.

- Open an application file running in its associated program.

The last operation is explained in more detail on the next page.
Consider the four sample files shown below in the Windows Explorer.

Customer list.mdb
Microsoft Access Application
332 KB

 Further Advance.doc
Microsoft Word Document
22 KB

 Monthly Accounts.xls
Microsoft Excel Worksheet
15 KB

 New logo.bmp
800 x 600
Bitmap Image

The associated program for each file is a program in which the file can be opened. In the above example, the **New logo** file is associated with Microsoft Paint and the **Monthly Accounts** spreadsheet is associated with Microsoft Excel.

For example, highlight the spreadsheet **Monthly Accounts** file in the Windows Explorer or My Computer. Then, depending on the mouse clicking option set in **Tools**, **Folder Options...**, **General** as described earlier, either click or double click over the icon or the filename. The spreadsheet program Microsoft Excel will start up, with the **Monthly Accounts** file open in its window.

Right-clicking

A quick way to access the menus (as an alternative to **File** and **Edit** on the menu bars) is to click the right mouse button over a file or (folder) in the Windows Explorer or My Computer. This produces the menu shown on the right. Right clicking on a gap on the Windows Taskbar on the bottom of the screen brings up a menu for "tiling" the screen windows. This enables folders to be displayed side-by-side and makes it easy to copy files between folders using "drag and drop". (Discussed shortly). Right-clicking the icon for a hard disc drive in My Computer is useful to examine the free space on the disc and to access the disc maintenance tools. (Described later in this book).

Saving Files in a Specified Location

A file is created every time you save a piece of work in an application such as Word, Excel or Paint. Using **File** and **Save As...** you can select the location where you want to save the work. The **Save As** window below shows the **C:** drive (usually the primary hard disc drive), the floppy disc drive **A:** and a re-writeable CD drive, which can be used for saving files.

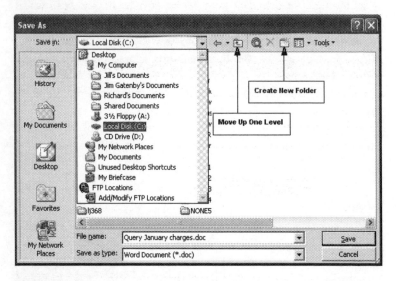

Note in the above **Save As** dialogue box, to move to a particular folder on the **C:** drive double click **Local Disk (C:)** then continue double clicking to work your way down through the folders and sub-folders. Similarly to move through the folders to disc level, click the **Up One Level** icon on the top row of the **Save As** dialogue box.

Please also note, as indicated in the above dialogue box, there is a **Create New Folder** icon to place a new folder in the currently selected folder or location.

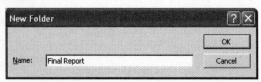

Saving Files on Another Computer

If you have a home network, you can use the **Save As** dialogue box to make a copy on another computer on the network. For example, I make a backup copy of all my work on the second machine on my home network. This is a very fast and convenient backup method and is used in addition to making regular copies on CD-R. Simply double click **My Network Places** as shown in the previous **Save As** dialogue, then select the required computer from the list of network resources which appears. Then select the required location (disc drive, folder, etc.) on the second computer, where a copy of your work is to be saved.

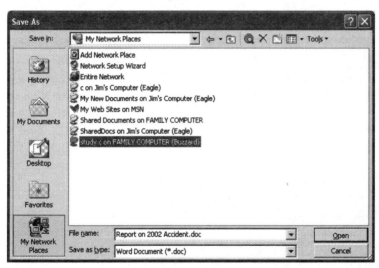

In the example above, the machine used to save the backup is the **FAMILY COMPUTER** with the unique identification of **Buzzard**. These are names invented when you first set up a home or small office network, as discussed later in this book.

Entering the Filename

You make up the name for a new file and enter it in the **File name:** bar at the bottom of the **Save As** window.

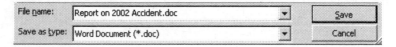

Windows XP permits long filenames (up to 255 characters). So you can give the file a meaningful name, such as **Report on 2002 Accident,** rather than **JIM1** for example. Using a meaningful name should help you to identify the document at a later date.

Selecting the File Type

When you save a file in Microsoft Word, for example, the file type will be automatically set as a Word Document (**.doc**) or whatever, depending on the program you are using. This is shown in the **Save as type:** bar at the bottom of the **Save As** window shown above. However, it is possible to specify a different file type by clicking the down arrow on the right of **Save as type:** bar. This reveals a choice of file formats in which the document can be saved. Scroll down the list to see the full range of file types, including various **Web Page** formats.

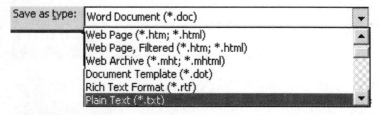

Text Files

The ability to save files in different formats makes it easier to transfer files between computers running different software. For example, saving a file in the **Plain Text (*.txt)** file type will produce a file in a simple but widely acceptable format which can be imported into a variety of software. This enables files produced using Microsoft Word, say, to be imported into computers using a different brand of word processor.

Options for Saving

Applications such as Word and Excel contain a range of options for saving files. For example, in Microsoft Word, selecting **File**, **Save As...**, then **Tools** and **General Options...** displays the following dialogue box:

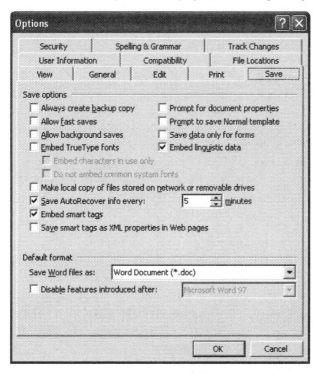

The option **Always create backup copy** makes a duplicate of the previous version of the document being saved. The backup has the file extension **.WBK** and is placed in the same folder as the main copy of the file. **Allow fast saves** only records the changes to a file. **Save AutoRecover info every:** allows you to recover your work on restarting Word after a power failure or machine crash, etc.

While producing an important document, it's a good idea to make a backup copy on a removable medium such as a floppy disc. Simply use the **Save As...** option and select **3½ Floppy (A:)** as the destination.

Creating Folders

The Windows Explorer and My Computer can both be used to create new folders in which to organize your work. The Windows Explorer has been used in the following example.

Suppose I want to start a new folder, **Building Project**, to hold files on some home improvements. I want to create the new folder within my existing folder **Home** which itself resides in **Gatenby's Folder** at the top level of the hierarchy on the **C:** drive.

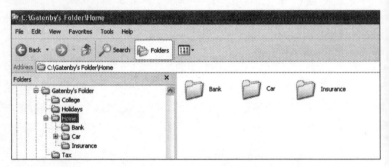

Start the Windows Explorer after right clicking over the **start** button. Highlight the **Home** folder into which the new folder is to be located. Select **File, New** and **Folder** and a **New Folder** will appear as shown below. Alternatively you can press the right-hand mouse button over an empty part of the Explorer right-hand window, then select **New** and **Folder** from the menu which appears.

The **File and Folders Tasks** menu, new in Windows XP and discussed shortly, may be displayed in a panel on the left-hand side of a folder window. This contains an option **Make a new folder**.

As can be seen previously, the **New Folder** has been placed alongside of the existing folders in the **Home** folder. The flashing cursor is used to delete the default name **New Folder** and replace with the chosen filename (**Building Project** in this example) as shown below.

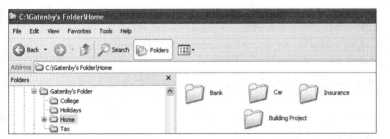

The left-hand panel below shows the new folder **Building Project** in the list of folders in the **Home** folder, which is itself in **Gatenby's Folder**. The full *path name* of a file in the **Building Project** folder would be:

C:\Gatenby's Folder\Home\Building Project

This is shown in the Windows Explorer window below:

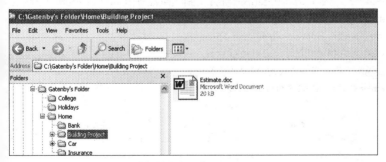

You can place new folders anywhere in your hierarchy of folders. Simply highlight the required "parent" folder which is to host the new folder, before selecting **File**, **New** and **Folder**. To place a new folder at the highest level of the hierarchy, open the Windows Explorer and make sure that your **C:** drive (or whatever) is highlighted before selecting **File**, **New** and **Folder**.

Common File and Folder Tasks

The next few pages discuss a number of methods for carrying out some of the most common tasks involved in managing your files and folders. Many of these tasks can also be carried out using the new **File and Folder Tasks** pane introduced in Windows XP and this is discussed in detail later in this chapter.

Renaming Files and Folders

This work can be carried out equally well in the Windows Explorer or in My Computer. A folder or file can be renamed by right clicking over its icon in My Computer or the Windows Explorer, then selecting **Rename** from the menu which appears (shown on the right). Alternatively the folder or filename can be highlighted, followed by selection of **File** and **Rename** from the menu bar across the top of the Explorer or My Computer window. The folder or filename appears in a rectangle with a flashing cursor. Rename the folder or file by deleting the existing name and typing in the new one, then press **Enter**.

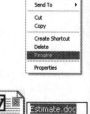

Deleting Files and Folders

Highlight the file or folder in the Windows Explorer or My Computer then press the **Delete** key. Or you can select **Delete** from the **File** menu. (The **File** menu can be invoked from the menu bar or by right clicking over the file or folder). When you delete a folder then all of the subfolders and files contained within are also deleted i.e. moved to the Recycle Bin. Unlike some earlier systems, Windows XP doesn't require a folder to be empty before it can be deleted.

Another way to delete files (in the Windows Explorer or My Computer) is to highlight the file or folder and select **Delete** from the **File and Folder Tasks** menu on the left of the screen, as shown on the next page. For this menu to appear, select **View**, **Explorer Bar** and make sure the word **Folders** is not ticked in the drop-down menu

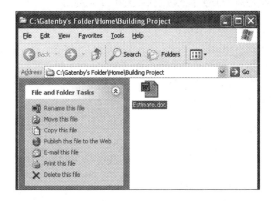

Undoing a Delete Operation

If you make a mistake and delete the wrong folders or files, you can use the **Undo Delete** option in the **Edit** menu (provided you spot the mistake straight away.) Fortunately files and folders are not lost forever when they are deleted. Windows XP merely transfers them to its **Recycle Bin**. Once in the Recycle Bin files and folders can be left for a time, but as they are still taking up hard disc space they should eventually be permanently deleted. There is also an option to restore files from the Recycle Bin to their original location on the hard disc.

The Recycle Bin

The Recycle Bin is invoked by clicking its icon on the Windows Desktop. It is effectively a folder into which all deleted files are initially sent. As shown below, you can view the contents of the Recycle Bin at any time by clicking its icon on the Windows Desktop.

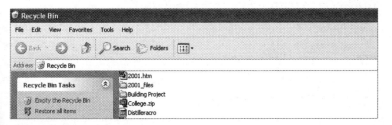

Files which have been "deleted" remain in the Recycle Bin until you decide to empty it. This is done by selecting **Empty the Recycle Bin** from the **Recycle Bin Tasks** shown in the previous screenshot or by selecting **File** then **Empty Recycle Bin** off the menu bar at the top of the Recycle Bin window. The Recycle Bin should be emptied regularly since files in the Recycle Bin are still taking up disc space. Individual files can also be highlighted and deleted.

Should you wish to reinstate files which have been consigned to the bin, open up the Recycle Bin window by clicking its icon on the Windows Desktop. Then highlight the file to be restored and select **Restore this item** from the **Recycle Bin Tasks**. Alternatively select **File** and **Restore** from the menu bar for the Recycle Bin. The files will be restored to their original locations on the hard disc.

Moving and Copying Files and Folders

The following tasks are described in the context of files, but the methods apply equally to folders.

Moving a file deletes the file from its original location and places it in a new location.

Copying a file places a replica of the file in a new location and leaves the original edition of the file in the original location.

Files may be copied or moved between different locations on the same hard disc, between two hard discs in the same computer or between different media such as hard and floppy discs.

If you have two or more computers on a network, files may be copied between them using **My Network Places** discussed later. It is common practice to make backup copies of important files by copying onto floppy discs, ZIP discs, writeable or rewriteable CD-ROMs and special backup tapes.

Dragging and Dropping

A common copying method is to drag the file or folder and drop it over the new location. Different results are obtained depending on whether you are dragging and dropping to the same or a different medium:

- The file is *moved* if it is dragged and dropped into a different location on the *same* hard disc.

- The file is *copied* if it is dragged and dropped onto a different disc drive.

- To *copy* files within the same hard disc the **Control** key must be held down while dragging with the left-hand mouse button.

Files and folders can be copied in the Windows Explorer or My Computer. You can copy between different locations on the main hard disc drive **C:** or to and from any other drives such as the floppy disc, ZIP disc, rewriteable (CD-RW) or secondary hard disc drives. Invoke the Windows Explorer and make sure the folders or files you wish to copy or move are visible in the right-hand panel. If you can't see the resources such as hard discs, floppy discs, etc., in the left-hand panel, select **View**, **Explorer Bar** and make sure **Folders** is ticked.

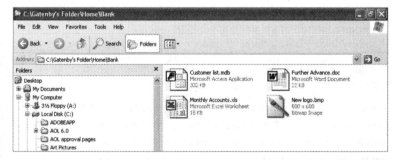

Now highlight the file(s) or folder(s) to be copied or moved. (To highlight multiple files and folders simultaneously, hold down the **Ctrl** key continuously while clicking with the mouse.) Next hold down the left-hand button and drag the highlighted files and/or folders to their destination in the left-hand panel. Release the mouse button to drop the files into the new location.

This method would typically be used to copy some files onto a floppy disc or CD to transfer them to another computer.

Using the Right-hand Mouse Button to Copy or Move Files

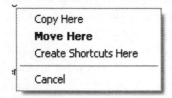

If you drag the icon for a file or folder using the *right* button on the mouse, then release the button to drop the file over its new location, the menu shown on the right appears, allowing you to select whether the file is to be moved or copied.

You can also copy and move files in the Windows Explorer or My Computer by using the **Edit** menus in the respective windows. Select the file(s) then use **Edit** and either **Copy** or **Cut** in the first (source) window followed by **Edit** and **Paste** in the destination window.

The File and Folder Tasks Menu

Windows XP has made many file and folder tasks much simpler. This has been done by the addition of the **File and Folder Tasks** pane on the left of the Windows Explorer and My Computer screens. The task pane, as shown below, can be switched on and off in Explorer or My Computer by clicking **View**, **Explorer Bar** and **Folders**. (The **File and Folder Tasks menu** alternates with the display of the hierarchy of folders).

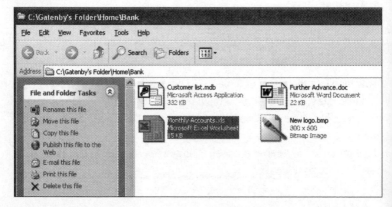

Please note that in the **File and Folder Tasks** pane, if a *file* is highlighted in the right-hand pane, a list of tasks appropriate to files appears in the task menu. This list is different from the task list which appears if a *folder* is highlighted. Apart from options to **Rename** and **Delete**, **E-mail** and **Publish on the Web**, files and folders can also be moved or copied very easily using the **File and Folder Tasks** pane. Moving or copying is made particularly easily, since a **Copy** or **Move** window appears allowing the destination to be selected, as shown below. This allows you to select a destination on any of the disc drives on the computer you are using. In addition, if you are connected to a network you can select **My Network Places** and move or copy a file or folder to another computer. There is also an option to create a new folder.

WARNING!

It is extremely easy to move files and folders around a hard disc. Many files are pronounced lost or deleted or "wiped" when they have in fact been moved to a different location.

The notes in this book on the copying, moving, deleting and renaming of files apply only to the **data** files and folders which **you have created**.

Under no circumstances should you attempt to move, copy, delete or rename any of the **program files** or folders in Windows, Office, Word, Excel, Access or any of the other applications. The computer expects to find the programs in specific locations and the effect of organizing **program files** into your own folders will be to render the computer useless.

Displaying Windows

It is sometimes convenient to arrange for two or more windows to be displayed on the screen at the same time when using My Computer. First you need to make sure that each folder opens up in its own window. This is set in **Tools** and **Folder Options...** and the **General** tab, as shown below.

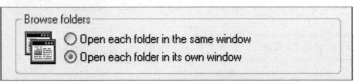

Make sure **Open each folder in its own window** is switched on as shown above then click **Apply** and **OK**.

Now open, in turn, each of the folders to be used in the copying or moving operation. At first the windows may not be clearly visible as they are in the *cascade* format, one behind another as shown in the next screenshot. Clicking anywhere on a folder brings it to the top of the cascade.

We now need to change from the cascade arrangement to the *tiling* display shown on the next page.

Tiling Windows

In this arrangement the windows are displayed in their entirety. To select tiling, move the cursor over an empty part of the Taskbar at the bottom of the Windows screen and click the right mouse button.

The Windows Taskbar

Right click over an empty space

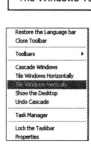

The menu on the left appears. If you select **Tile Windows Vertically**, any windows which are currently open will be displayed in the arrangement shown on the next page. To return to the cascade arrangement, right click again over an empty space on the Windows Taskbar and select **Cascade Windows** from the menu.

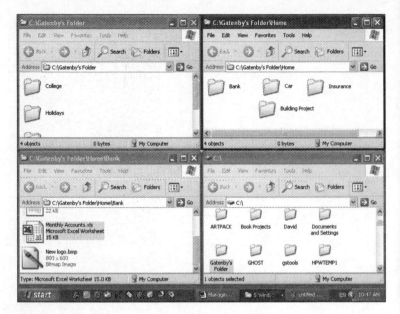

Displaying windows in the Tile configuration makes it easy to copy and move files and folders. The source and destination of the files or folders may be the same or different disc drives or different computers in the case of a network.

Copying Extracts Between Programs

The Tiling arrangement can be used to copy an extract from a document or drawing running in a window in one program and paste into another program. In the example which follows, Word and Paint are simultaneously running in separate windows, each displaying an open file. To copy an extract from one program to another:

- Select or highlight the extract which is to be copied.

- Next select **File** and **Copy** from the menu bar. This places the extract on the *clipboard* - a temporary storage area.

- Now change to the second window and place the cursor at the point where the extract is to be inserted.

- Select **File** and **Paste** to place the extract in its new position.

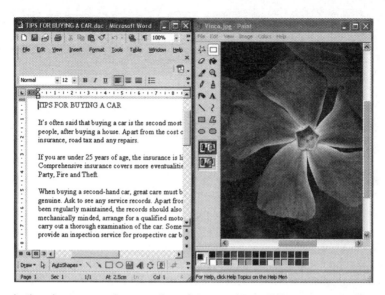

In the above example, a section of the graphic in Paint in the right-hand window could be cut and pasted into the text in Word in the left-hand window.

Finding Files and Folders

Even if your work is organized into a system of clearly labelled folders, there are still occasions when you need help to locate files and folders. Windows XP provides a search facility which scans selected disc drives then displays a list of any locations where the required files or folders have been found. You can initiate the search process from the menus using **start**, **Search** and **All files and folders**.

Enter all or part of the name of the required file or folder. Alternatively you can use the *wildcard* asterisk (*) to replace any letters you are not sure of or do not want to type. For example, ***.exe** will search for all files which end in the **.exe** extension.

The result of a search for a folder called **Car Accident** is shown below.

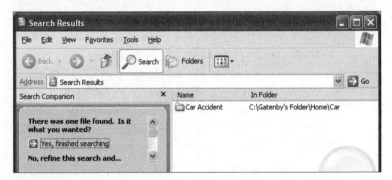

There are options to accept the results of the search or to repeat the search with refined criteria. Various options for the new criteria appear when you move the scroll bar in the left-hand panel shown above. The right-hand panel shows the location of the required folder **Car Accident** which resides in the folder **Car**, shown with its full path name:

C:\Gatenby's Folder\Home\Car

Double clicking on the file or folder name in the right-hand panel opens up the folder in its own window.

Creating a Shortcut Icon on the Windows Desktop

To save time locating and opening frequently used files and folders, you can place a shortcut icon on the Windows Desktop. First highlight the file or folder in the Windows Explorer or My Computer. Now right click over the file or folder and select **Send To** and **Desktop (create shortcut)** from the menu shown right. The file or folder can then be accessed by clicking the new shortcut icon on the

Windows Desktop. You can

Shortcut to
Car

Rename or **Delete** the shortcut icon after right clicking over the icon on the Windows Desktop.

Summary: Managing Files and Folders

- A file is a piece of work which has been saved on a disc. Windows XP permits filenames of up to 255 letters, so that meaningful names can be used.

- Files are created when you save your work in applications such as Word and Excel. These are generally referred to as documents or data files. Different applications produce different types of file and these are identified with their own filename *extension* such as **.doc** or **.xls**.

- The programs or applications which you run, such as Word and Excel, contain many special files. These are known as program files (with extensions such as **.exe**) and these files must not be moved, modified or deleted by the user.

- Windows XP has been designed to allow the user to organise files easily into folders and subfolders. Use the folder **My Documents**, provided by Windows, to save your work until you are ready to create your own hierarchy of folders and subfolders.

- Files have attributes which may be changed by the user. These include **Read Only** to prevent the file from being accidentally deleted, and **Hidden** to disguise the presence of the file. The **Archive** attribute marks the file as needing to be backed up.

- Both My Computer and the Windows Explorer provide facilities to manage your work including creating folders, copying, moving, deleting and renaming files and folders.

- The **Save As...** option, in applications such as Word and Excel, allows you to specify a saving location for a file. The location may be a particular folder or subfolder on your main hard disc (usually the C: drive). Alternatively a different disc drive such as a floppy disc, ZIP drive, CD-ROM or a second hard disc drive may be specified.

- Files which are deleted are sent to the Windows XP Recycle Bin. There is an option to restore files in the Recycle Bin to their original location. However, files in the Recycle Bin must be permanently deleted if disc space is to be saved.

- Windows XP introduces the **File and Folder Tasks** panel, which appears on the left-hand side of a window in My Computer or the Windows Explorer. This provides a menu of options for managing files and folders, including **Rename**, **Move**, **Copy** and **Delete**.

- Most file and folder tasks can also be accomplished by simple mouse operations such as "dragging" and "dropping" or by selecting options from the **File** and **Edit** menus.

- A safe way to manipulate files and folders is to drag and drop using the right-hand button then select the required copy or move operation from the small menu which appears.

- Care should be taken when moving files: *program files* should never be moved. Accidental moving of files (when copying is intended) may result in the loss of important work.

- The Windows **Search** option allows you to search for files and folders using the full name of the file or folder. You can also use part of the name and one or more wildcard characters (*) to replace any unknown letters. Files which contain a specified piece of text within the document can also be found.

- A shortcut icon can be placed on the Windows Desktop, giving direct access to frequently used files and folders. This is quicker than locating the file or folder in Windows Explorer or My Computer.

Hard Disc Care

Introduction

The hard disc drive inside of your computer is home to your most valuable computing assets - the software or programs which run the computer and the data files representing your hours of toil. So it's essential to keep the hard disc running reliably and at peak efficiency.

In fact, hard disc drives are extremely reliable given that they are mechanical devices which rotate at several thousand rpm. Out of a few hundred machines with which I have been acquainted, only a handful ever needed a replacement hard disc unit. However, the integrity of the program and data files stored on the magnetic surfaces of hard discs is another matter. Apart from the risk of viruses (covered in detail in a later chapter), the software and data files on the hard disc can be corrupted in a number of ways. It is therefore not unusual to have to carry out "repairs" or even a complete formatting and re-installation of the program and data files on the hard disc.

Some of these problems can be avoided by careful maintenance or good "housekeeping". For example, as a hard disc drive becomes full, the computer gradually runs more slowly before finally grinding to a halt, when there is no room left to store the temporary files needed to run large applications. This can be avoided by regularly deleting redundant programs and files.

Windows XP provides a battery of utilities for maintaining your computer. Some of them were available in earlier versions of Windows, while others had to be purchased from third-party software companies.

The following pages describe some of the main utilities which Windows XP provides for maintaining your hard disc.

Examining Your Hard Disc

There are several ways of gaining access to the tools for maintaining your hard disc. One method is to open **My Computer** and right click over the icon for the hard disc drive (normally the **C:** drive). From the menu which appears select **Properties**. As shown below, the **Properties** dialogue box for the **C:** drive appears. This gives details of the used and free space on the hard disc. Similar information is also given on the **System Tasks** pane on the left-hand side of **My Computer**.

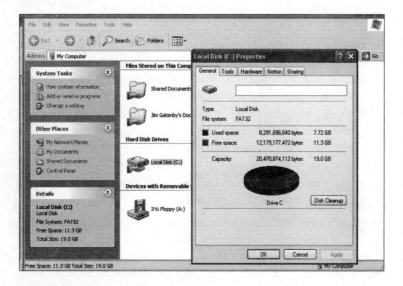

The **Disk Cleanup** feature, accessed by the button shown above on the right, enables you to delete unwanted files from the hard disc. These include temporary files and debris left over from surfing the Internet, as shown in the **Disk Cleanup** window on the next page. Click **OK** to remove the redundant files and create more free space on the hard disc drive.

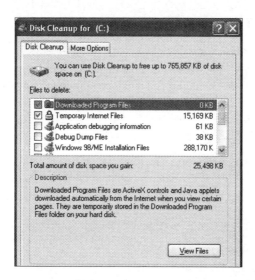

If you select the **More Options** tab shown on the right above, the following menu appears, allowing you to remove redundant *software* i.e. programs, rather than the Internet debris and temporary files shown above.

Removing Windows Components

Windows components include software in the **Accessories** menu
(**start** and **All Programs**) such as **Paint** and **Notepad**. Clicking **Clean
up…**under **Windows components** shown in the previous **Disk
Cleanup** window opens the **Windows Components Wizard** below.
This allows you to delete any of the features in Windows XP which you
no longer use. Windows components can also be *installed* using this
feature.

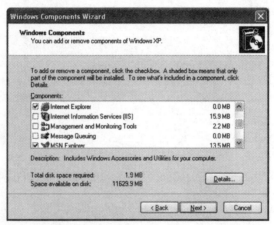

Removing Installed Programs

Installed programs shown in the **Disk Cleanup** window at the bottom
of the previous page refers to applications packages such as word
processors, spreadsheets, graphics, games, etc., which are not part of
the Windows XP operating system. These are usually programs that
have been added to your computer after Windows XP was installed,
either by the suppliers of your computer or by yourself.

To delete a major software package, it's not simply a case of deleting
the folders bearing the name of the program, listed in My Computer or
the Windows Explorer. Large programs usually have lots of other files
and settings scattered about the system. Failure to delete all of the
associated files may cause problems or at least display some irritating
error messages.

Many programs, such as Adobe Acrobat for example, have an integral option to uninstall. This is accessed from **start**, **All Programs** then the name of the program. Selecting **Uninstall Adobe Acrobat 4.0** in the menu shown below should remove the program and all of its associated files.

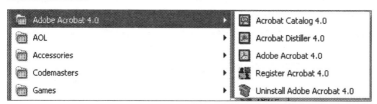

If a piece of software doesn't have its own uninstall feature as shown above then use the Windows XP **Add or Remove Programs** feature shown below. This is launched from the **Disk Cleanup** window shown on page 53, by selecting the **Clean up...** button under **Installed programs**. This feature can also be accessed from **start**, **Control Panel** (in **Category View**) and **Add or Remove Programs**.

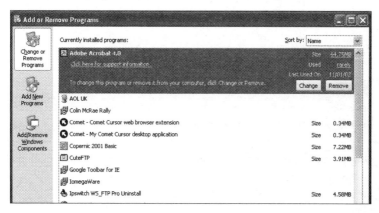

To remove a program, highlight its entry and click the **Remove** button. The **Add or Remove Programs** window shown above also includes icons on the left-hand side giving access to the **Add New Progams** and **Add/Remove Windows Components** features.

The Tools Menu

Referring to the **Local Disk(C:) Properties** window shown on page 52, clicking the **Tools** tab displays buttons for the **Error-checking**, **Defragmentation** and **Backup** features of Windows XP as shown below.

Error-checking of the Hard Disc

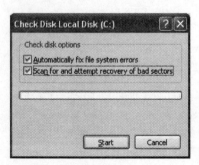

This feature scans the hard disc and corrects any corrupt data or program files. Scans should be carried out regularly to keep your hard disc working efficiently. Windows XP allows routine tasks such as error-checking scans to be scheduled at regular times in the week (discussed later).

Defragmenting the Hard Disc

This option appears in the middle of the **Tools** tab of the **Local Disk(C:) Properties** window shown on the previous page.

Defragmention rearranges commonly used programs and their essential files so that they are all located on the hard disc in close proximity (said to be "contiguous" or "touching"). This makes the applications run faster.

The previous features were accessed by highlighting the hard disc (C: drive) in **My Computer** then selecting **Properties** and **Tools** after right clicking the disc drive icon. Alternatively select **File**, **Properties** and **Tools** in **My Computer**.

Using the Control Panel

Many of these maintenance tools can also be launched from the **Control Panel** listed on the **start** menu. The **Control Panel** is shown in the **Category View** on the next page. The menu on the left of the **Control Panel** allows you to switch between **Category View** and the **Classic View** associated with earlier versions of Microsoft Windows.

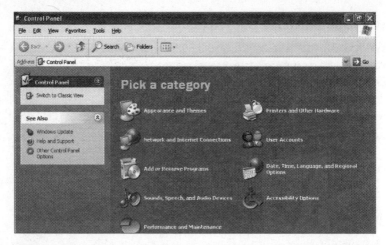

Notice in the above window that you can access the **Add or Remove Programs** feature discussed earlier, in the section on **Disk Cleanup**. Also visible at the bottom is the **Performance and Maintenance** option which leads to the window shown below. Apart from including the **Disk Cleanup** and defragmentation features discussed earlier, this window gives access to **Scheduled Tasks** allowing maintenance tasks to be carried out automatically at programmed times in the week. **Back up your data** is discussed later in this book in a separate chapter.

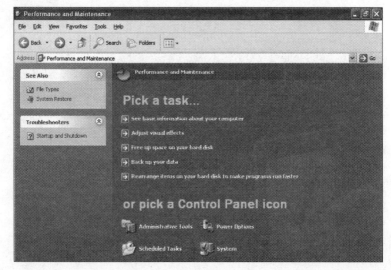

Windows Update

Windows Update is intended to ensure that you always have the latest versions of drivers and software "fixes" installed on your hard disc. To use Windows Update you must be connected to the Internet, since its resources are drawn from a Microsoft Web site. You can start **Windows Update** from the menu shown on the right, obtained after clicking **start** and **Control Panel**.

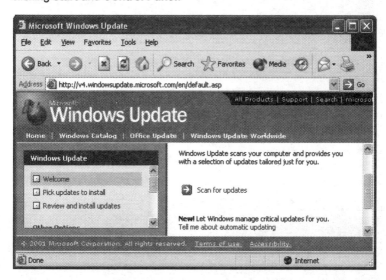

Once on-line to the Internet site, your hard disc is examined to see what software and device drivers are installed. If later versions do exist, you can choose to download them from the Internet and install them on your machine's hard disc.

Windows Update can also be set to download new versions of software automatically. This is done by selecting **start**, **Control Panel** then double clicking the **System** icon. (If necessary switch to the **Classic View** of the **Control Panel**). Click the **Automatic Updates** tab to see the options.

System Restore

The purpose of System Restore is to allow you to repair your system if any of the important system settings are corrupted. This might happen when installing a new piece of software or hardware, for example. The idea is that you take regular snapshots of the critical settings. Then if things go wrong you can retrieve an earlier, healthy configuration. The snapshots or **restore points** are taken automatically by the system at regular intervals. Alternatively you can create restore points manually.

Launch **System Restore** from **start**, **Control Panel**, **Performance and Maintenance** and then **System Restore** from the menu shown on the left.

You are given a choice to either use a previous restore point or create a new one. Click **Next** and you are presented with one of two screens. If you opted to use an existing restore point, then you are given a calendar from which to choose a previous configuration which you know to be good. The dates when restore points were created are shown in bold.

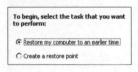

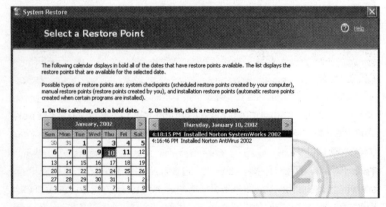

Click **Next** to restore the selected configuration.

Scheduling Routine Tasks

Routine tasks can be scheduled to run automatically at convenient times daily, weekly or monthly for example. **Scheduled Tasks** can be launched from **start**, **Control Panel** and the **Performance and Maintenance** menu as shown on the right. Or you can select **start**,

All Programs, **Accessories**, **System Tools** and **Scheduled Tasks**.

The main **Scheduled Tasks** window is shown below.

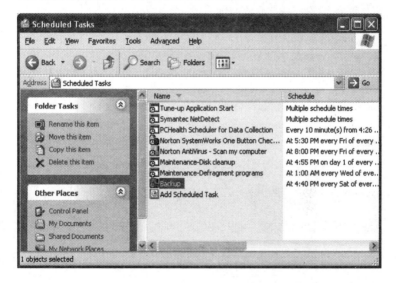

Scheduling is used for routine maintenance tasks, such as error-checking of the hard drive, defragmentation and virus checking (discussed later).

To schedule a new task, double click on **Add Scheduled Task** as shown in the above screenshot. This launches the **Scheduled Task Wizard** shown on the next page.

Click **Next** to leave the introductory screen and you are presented with a list of programs from which you select the one(s) to be scheduled.

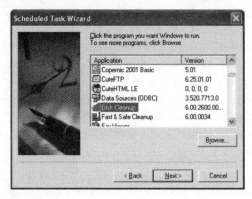

In the above example I have selected **Disk Cleanup** to be scheduled. Clicking **Next** enables you to work through the **Scheduled Task Wizard** to specify the frequency, day and time when the program is to run automatically. A common use of scheduling is to leave computers running overnight and schedule backup copying of important files in the middle of the night when the computers are not being used.

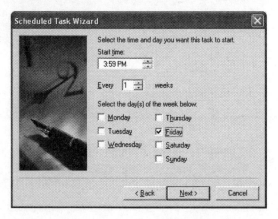

You are required to enter your password before clicking **Finish** to include the new task in the list of scheduled tasks.

Using Hard Disc Space as Extra Memory – Paging Files

When Windows XP is working away on memory hungry applications, it uses part of the hard disc to supplement the memory or RAM chips (SIMMs). This "virtual memory" takes the form of a *paging file* (also known as a *swap file*) on the hard disc. You can look at the virtual memory of your computer by selecting **start,** then double clicking on the **System** icon in the **Control Panel**, which should be open in **Classic View**. Click the **Advanced** tab and under **Performance** click **Settings** and **Advanced**. When you click the **Change** button under the heading **Virtual memory**, the **Virtual Memory** dialogue box appears, as shown below.

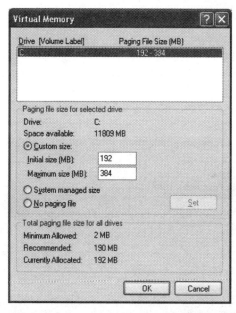

You may increase the paging file, if necessary, when running very large programs. It is advisable not to *decrease* the paging file below the recommended minimum of 1.5 times the size of the RAM (or memory chips) installed in your computer. Virtual memory is also accessible via the **Systems** icon in the **Performance and Maintenance** feature of the **Control Panel** in **Category View**.

Norton SystemWorks

Norton
SystemWorks

A number of companies make third party software to augment the components already provided in Windows XP. The Norton range of utility software from Symantec is well-established and very successful. Norton SystemWorks 2002 has been designed to work with Windows XP and contains a number of powerful utilities which are also available for purchase as separate programs. These utilities are designed to optimize the running of your computer by keeping the hard disc operating at peak efficiency and free from viruses. The Norton AntiVirus program included in Norton SystemWorks is discussed separately later in this book.

A brief overview of some of the main components of Norton SystemWorks is given below:

Norton CleanSweep

This program identifies and removes redundant files and programs on your hard disc.

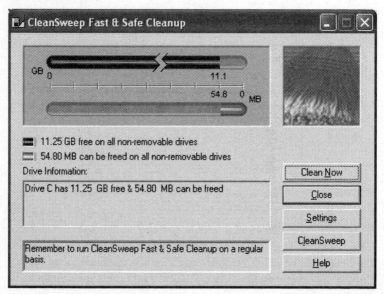

Norton CleanSweep can also remove temporary Internet files including "cookies". Cookies contain information relating to Web sites and they can safely be removed, although this may mean that, for example, personal information required for on-line purchases may need to be re-entered if you revisit a Web site.

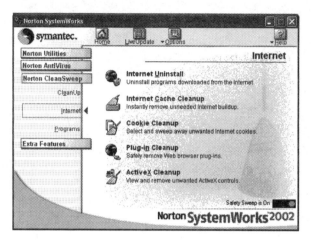

Uninstall Wizard

This is part of Norton CleanSweep and allows you to select and uninstall any programs you no longer use.

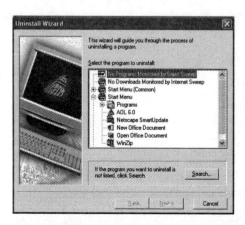

Norton Disk Doctor

This is a part of the Norton Utilities suite of programs which is included with Norton SystemWorks. Its purpose is to scan the surface of the hard disc and repair any problems.

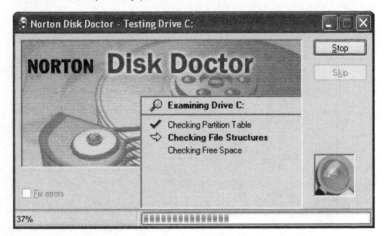

Speed Disk

This program is similar to the defragmenter in Windows XP and is designed to make programs run faster. Performance is improved by reorganising files so that they are less scattered over the disc surface.

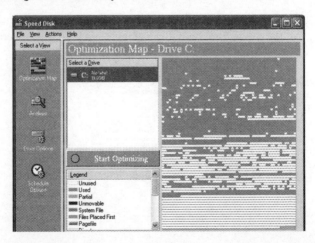

Summary: Hard Disc Care

- Many maintenance activities are aimed at maximising the free space on your hard disc. This is necessary not only to accommodate new software and data files but also to keep the computer running at its optimum performance.

- The Paging File (Virtual Memory) uses free disc space to supplement the actual memory consisting of banks of RAM chips.

- The amount of free space on a disc drive can be examined by highlighting the drive in **My Computer**. The **Tools** tab (**File** and **Properties)** presents various maintenance features for error checking and deleting redundant files and software.

- After a time, files can become fragmented on the hard disc and cause the system to slow down. Windows XP uses defragmentation to reorganise files and compact the disc free space.

- Error-checking is a process which scans the disc and corrects errors in files and on the disc surfaces. Errors may typically be caused when there is a break in the power supply, or a system crash due to a fault in a program.

- Redundant programs, temporary files and unwanted Windows XP components should be deleted regularly to maximise free disc space. This can be done manually or with the help of Disk Cleanup.

- Maintenance tasks such as error checking and Disk Cleanup can be scheduled to run automatically at regular times on certain days of the week.

- Some packages contain their own uninstall facility in their list of components in the **Programs** menu. This should enable all files related to a package to be removed without leaving any debris behind.

- Deleted files are automatically sent to the Recycle Bin, which is itself a folder on the hard disc. Therefore to increase free disc space, the Recycle Bin must be emptied.

- Windows Update is a Windows XP utility which uses an Internet site to carry out an audit of your hard disc. If appropriate, newer versions of programs and device drivers can be downloaded to your hard disc. Technical support is also available from the Internet site.

- System Restore saves regular snapshots of the critical settings and systems files in your computer. If faults develop you can retrieve and install a previous configuration which was saved when the system was working properly.

- Third party software provides a lot of additional utilities to keep your computer and hard disc running at peak efficiency. Norton SystemWorks 2002 includes the well-known Norton Utilities together with Norton CleanSweep and Norton AntiVirus. Also included in SystemWorks is the GoBack feature for restoring your computer to an earlier, healthy configuration.

Please Note:

In order to keep your hard disc and its valuable contents safe, the maintenance tasks detailed in this chapter should be combined with a strategy for regular backing up and virus testing of all discs and files as described elsewhere in this book. If your machine is used for serious work, the data files on your hard disc are probably worth far more than the entire computer and its associated peripheral hardware devices.

Backup Activities

Introduction

If your computer is used for any sort of serious work, then backing up is one of the most important (but frequently neglected) tasks to be performed. Imagine working on a project for several weeks or months then suddenly losing all of the files. The result is exactly the same as someone breaking into a filing cabinet and stealing important documents or a fire which sweeps through a building. The difference is that it's very easy to lose a file or folder saved on a hard disc. As a teacher, I frequently heard remarks like "The stupid computer has wiped my work…". A moment's carelessness when copying or deleting files or a system crash can easily destroy hours of work.

While small files like a letter or simple spreadsheet can be created again very easily, this is not the case with, for example, a student dissertation, a design project or a set of accounts accumulated over a long period. In many cases the value of the data files stored on the hard disc will be far in excess of the value of the computer hardware.

So it makes sense to devise a strategy for making regular backups i.e. duplicate copies of your work. Several methods are discussed later in this chapter and these are inexpensive in relation to the cost and inconvenience caused by serious data loss.

Apart from the data files representing hours of toil, your hard disc contains all of the systems software such as the Windows XP operating system and applications like Microsoft Office. If necessary, software can be restored from the original CDs and floppy discs. It's essential that all of your original software packages (including CDs, discs and any documentation) are carefully stored in a safe place.

What is Memory?

The Hard Disc Drive is the main medium for keeping *permanent* copies of your work; it corresponds to the filing cabinet in the traditional office. In order to put the hard disc in context we must first be clear about its role in the operation of the computer.

Many new computer users are confused by the term "memory". When the computer gives an "out of memory..." error, for example, some users mistakenly believe their hard disc is full. In fact, this error refers to the capacity of the microchips which form the computer's memory.

Types of Storage

There are two main ways of storing data:

- Temporary storage in the computer's memory.
- Permanent storage by recording on a magnetic medium such as the hard disc (and also floppy discs, tape, ZIP discs and writeable CD-ROM).

The Memory

The memory (also known as RAM - Random Access Memory) consists of several banks of microchips, known as SIMMs. The memory is a temporary store for the programs and data currently being used. Any data which is typed in the computer will sit in the memory until:

- You switch the computer off, or
- The data is overwritten by new data which you have typed in or loaded from disc.

Saving Your Work

The memory is said to be *volatile*, i.e. its contents are lost when the power is removed. In order to keep a permanent copy of the data it should be saved on the hard disc or other magnetic storage medium. Some software has an option to perform a background save at regular

 intervals (set by the user). Alternatively, it's a simple matter to click the save icon from time to time, for example every 15 minutes.

The Hard Disc Drive

The hard disc drive is a sealed unit built inside of the computer and physically inaccessible unless you remove the computer's metal casing. The magnetic disc surfaces (platters) on which programs and data are recorded are an integral part of the drive unit, which also contains the moving heads used for reading and writing data.

The hard disc is usually designated as the **C:** drive, and consists of a set of metal discs coated in a magnetic material and rotating about a central spindle. The hard disc unit is housed in a metal case and is sealed to prevent particles of dust from entering and damaging the disc surfaces, which are machined to very fine tolerances.

In normal use the hard disc rotates at several thousand revolutions per minute, making it a very high performance device but also vulnerable to catastrophic failures. If the moving head which "reads" the data from the disc touches one of the disc surfaces (resulting in a "head crash"), the disc surface will be scratched and some, if not all, of the data will be lost. (A head crash might be caused, for example, by moving or bumping the computer while the hard disc is running.)

The Contents of the Hard Disc Drive

Permanently saved on the magnetic surfaces of the hard disc are the programs and data files essential for the running of your computer. The hard disc is not to be confused with the memory or RAM of the computer, which is the temporary store used to hold programs and data while they are in current use. When you switch the computer off the contents of the RAM are cleared, but the contents of the hard disc remain in place. The hard disc normally contains:

- The *systems* software such as the Windows XP operating system needed to start and run the computer.

- The *applications* software such as your word-processor, database, DTP, graphics or games.

- The work you have produced and saved as files - the word processing documents, spreadsheets, graphics files, music, etc.

The hard disc is generally a robust component which can perform reliably for many thousands of hours over several years. However, due to possible accidents and natural disasters, it is by no means uncommon for individuals and companies to "lose" the entire contents of a hard disc.

In some cases the files of data may still reside on the disc after a disaster, but the user loses the ability to retrieve them by normal methods. (There are companies specialising in the recovery of data from damaged hard discs but this can be an expensive process).

With a hard disc drive you really have got "all of your eggs in one basket". If the hard disc fails without adequate backup arrangements, your computer will be useless. This can spell disaster for a small business.

Ways to Lose Your Data

- The computer or some of its internal components such as the hard disc drive may be stolen.

- You may accidentally delete important files by giving the wrong command.

- Someone may deliberately wipe or format the entire disc.

- The data on the hard disc may be corrupted by a software error or a failure in the power supply.

- The data may be damaged by one of the many computer viruses which can attack your system from various sources, such as a malicious e-mail.

- The hard disc may be damaged by the spilling of drinks or the data corrupted by exposure to a magnetic field after placing it near to another electrical device such as a stereo speaker.

- The computer itself may be totally destroyed by events such as fire, flood, earthquake or explosion.

- After several years' faithful service, the hard disc may reach the end of its useful life.

Your Exposure to Risk

You can assess your exposure to risk by considering the following factors:

- How long would it take to completely restore your system in the event of a total hard disc failure? Consider the time needed for retyping documents and data entry.

- Could you re-install all of the essential software? Do you have the technical expertise? Can you quickly find all of the installation discs and CDs? (Driver software which enables hardware devices to function can be particularly elusive in times of crisis).

- Does the hard disc hold essential business files - customer records, accounts or CAD files, etc? If so, would the business grind to a halt if a major hard disc failure occurred.

- Have you spent months typing in your magnum opus, perhaps a dissertation or a new novel? If disaster struck, you wouldn't be the first author to lose the only copy of a 300 page tome.

- What about your Curriculum Vitae, which has been polished and updated over time, into the masterpiece it is today? The day your CV gets wiped is likely to be the time when you want to apply for a new job, and time may be critical.

- Who else uses the computer - might they damage files accidentally or deliberately? Does the business computer on which your livelihood depends also double up as the family games machine? Children are notorious for experimenting with settings and installing troublesome software.

- Does anyone import dubious files from floppy disc or the Internet which might spread viruses or wipe the hard disc?

The Backup Process

A good way to reduce the risk of a computing catastrophe is to make duplicate or backup copies of all important files. A backup is a copy of some or all of the files from a hard disc drive onto another "non-volatile" storage medium, such as a floppy disc, ZIP disc, CD or tape. (Non-volatile means the data is permanently saved after the computer is switched off - unlike data in the memory, which is lost when the power is removed.)

The purpose of a *full* backup is to allow a computer system and particularly its software and data files, to be completely recovered in the event of a total disaster, including the loss of the computer itself.

For important files, the backup discs or other storage media such as writeable CD and tape cartridges should be kept in a safe and secure place, away from heat and magnetic fields and preferably in a separate geographical location away from the computer. This also applies to the original installation discs and CD-ROMs from which software may need to be re-installed.

Although it is convenient to make backup copies onto another part of the same hard disc, these are of little use if the hard disc is damaged or the computer is stolen. Making backups on the same hard disc only gives protection against the deletion of some of the files.

For important work, a planned backup strategy is essential, with a system of several discs or tapes used in rotation. For a small backup consisting of a few important files, one or more floppy discs may be adequate to store the data. Alternatively, a full backup will copy the entire contents of the hard disc onto a writeable CD or special high capacity magnetic tape cartridge.

Capacities of Magnetic Storage Media

In order to determine the type of backup storage medium required for a particular task, you need to be familiar with the way data is represented in a computer and the units used to measure storage capacities. Then you can estimate the amount of space required to back up a particular set of files.

The basic unit of computer storage is the *byte*. This is the amount of space taken up by one character when it is temporarily stored in the computer's memory or permanently saved on a disc. A character is typically a letter of the alphabet (both upper and lower case), a punctuation mark or keyboard symbol, or a digit in the range 0-9.

Every character is represented in the computer by a code made up of eight binary digits. The binary code employs only the digits 0 and 1 and is used because it is relatively simple for an electronic device like a computer to represent two states. (This system can be demonstrated by a light bulb, representing 1 when it is switched on and 0 when it is off).

Examples of character codes used are as follows:

Character	Binary Code
A	0 1 0 0 0 0 0 1
a	0 1 1 0 0 0 0 1
9	0 0 1 1 1 0 0 1

The fact that computers perform their internal work using the binary system based on the number 2, rather than our normal decimal system based on 10, gives rise to some rather strange units for large numbers of bytes. The most common units used for describing computer capacities are the kilobyte, the megabyte and the gigabyte.

1 kilobyte (K) is approximately 1000 bytes (1024 to be exact)

1 megabyte (MB) is approximately 1000K or about a
million   bytes (1,048,576 to be exact)

1 gigabyte (GB) is approximately 1000 megabytes.

A kilobyte represents about a third of a page of text on A4 paper. If you include pictures and scanned images amongst the text of a document, the amount of storage space required increases rapidly. At the time of writing, files saved on disc are usually stated in kilobytes or megabytes and the memory or RAM is given in megabytes. The capacities of older hard disc drives are generally quoted in megabytes while the size of newer drives is stated in gigabytes.

Capacities of Different Storage Media

The table below shows some typical values for the size of currently available storage media.

Medium	Typical Storage Capacity
3.5 inch Floppy Diskette	1.44MB (uncompressed)
Hard Disc Drive	500 - 120000MB (120GB)
Tape Cartridge	4 - 500GB
CD-ROM	650MB
ZIP/Jaz Drive Discs	100MB, 250MB, 2GB

Choosing a Backup Medium

The 3.5 inch Floppy Diskette

Some people mistakenly think that the 3.5 inch disc, because of its rigid plastic case, is actually a "hard" disc. In fact, the magnetic disc material (known as the "cookie") inside the plastic case of the 3.5 inch disc is really quite flexible and "floppy".

The 3.5 inch diskette is portable and very easily inserted into or removed from the floppy disc drive (normally drive **A:**). In the past, most new software packages were supplied on one or more floppy discs. Now, with the increased size of new packages, this role has been taken over by the CD-ROM. Transferring data from a single CD is much faster and less prone to errors than from a large number of 3.5 inch diskettes.

However, the 3.5 inch disc is still a very cheap and convenient way of transferring a few files or a small piece of software from one computer to another. For example, if you want to save a document then take it home and carry on working on it. It's also a quick way to make a backup copy of an important file for security purposes.

Removable Hard Discs - ZIP Drives

These have the capacity of a small hard disc drive combined with the portability of a floppy disc. Two popular systems are the Iomega ZIP and Jaz drives. The smaller ZIP drive takes removable discs of 100MB capacity and there is also a 250MB version. The Jaz drive is the ZIP drive's bigger relative, with a capacity of 2GB.

I used an Iomega ZIP drive for about 3 years and found it to be extremely reliable and useful. While not having the capacity for a full system backup of a large hard disc (for which a tape cartridge is needed), the ZIP drive nevertheless has many valuable functions. It is many times faster than a tape drive and is therefore ideal for quick backups of software and data files which are too large for floppy discs.

The text and screenshots for a substantial book can fit comfortably on one ZIP disc without compression. To make similar backup copies with floppy discs would require a large number of "floppies" and a lot of time spent swapping discs in the floppy disc drive.

With your important data files copied onto ZIP discs and the essential software safe on its original CDs, you should be able to recover from a hard disc disaster.

After you install a ZIP drive for the first time, an icon for the drive appears in My Computer alongside of the other disc drives.

The ZIP drive can be treated like any of the other disc drives. This means it can be opened up in its own folder by double clicking its icon in My Computer. All the usual Windows XP operations, like copying and moving files by dragging and dropping in the Windows Explorer, can be performed. This enables files to be copied between the ZIP disc and any of the other disc drives.

There is also a set of Iomega ZIP Tools providing additional features. These include options to **Format...** the ZIP disc and to **Protect...** the disc with a password.

To save your work on the ZIP drive in applications like Word, you simply click **File** and **Save As...** then select the drive letter which the ZIP drive installation software has allocated. This could be either **D:**, **E:**, or **F:**, for example, depending on what hard drives and CD-ROM drives your machine contains.

The external version of the Iomega ZIP drive is particularly handy for transferring large files and software to other computers. You just plug the ZIP drive's cable into the printer port on the other machine and install the driver. A version of the ZIP drive is available which plugs into the USB port.

Compact Disc as a Backup Medium

Although CDs have been around for a long time, only in the last few years has it been possible, at an affordable price, to write and rewrite your own CDs. The CD-RW drive is similar in appearance to the earlier "read only" CD-ROM drives and is available in internal and external versions.

There are two main types of writeable CD media:

The **CD-R** disc can be written to only once, after which it can only be used for reading operations. CD-R discs currently cost around 50p.

The **CD-RW** disc can be used repeatedly for writing and rewriting. First it must be formatted to prepare it for the recording process, known as "Packet Writing". This allows the CD-RW disc to be used like a floppy or hard disc, with drag and drop copying operations, etc. CD-RW discs are currently priced at around £1 each. If you buy a CD-RW drive, it can be used to read normal data and audio CD-ROMs, to "burn" CD-R discs in a once only operation, and to format, write and rewrite CD-RWs.

Advertisements for CD-RW drives normally state performance in terms of writing, rewriting and reading speeds. For example, **24/10/40** means:

>Writes at 24 speed (3600KB/s)

>Rewrites at 10 speed (1500KB/s)

>Reads at 40 speed (6000KB/s)

Some CD-RW discs are claimed to be usable for at least a 1000 write operations. CD-RW drives have their own memory buffer to keep a constant flow of data to the disc during writing operations. Buffer sizes of 2 or 4MB are typical. Some CD-RW drives have a technology known as Burn-Proof to prevent breaks in the recording process, which can ruin CDs.

Before attempting to burn a CD-R it is worth checking the settings for the CD drive in **My Computer**. Right click over the icon for the CD drive and select **Properties** from the resulting menu. Now click the **Recording** tab to reveal the following dialogue box:

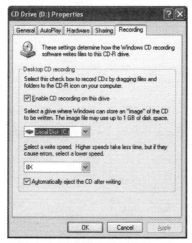

Make sure **Enable CD recording on this drive** is ticked. Note the speed (**8X**) at the bottom. This can be adjusted later if there are errors in recording. The "image" file referred to in the above window is created on your hard disc prior to the actual CD writing process. It contains all of the data to be written to the CD.

Burning a CD

This is a once only write operation, producing a CD-R which cannot be overwritten by dragging and dropping files or normal saving operations. Previous versions of Windows did not include CD burning software, so it was necessary to purchase a third party product. Two of the most popular packages are Easy CD Creator from Roxio (formerly Adaptec) and Nero from Ahead Software. The CD burning software built into Windows XP is provided by Roxio, although not including all of the advanced features of the full Easy CD Creator package. However, the Windows XP CD burning software is capable of copying data files to a CD and is therefore a useful backup tool. (Using Windows XP to create *audio* CDs is discussed later in the chapter on Windows Media Player).

Using Windows XP's Own CD Burning Software

Open **My Computer** and double click the hard disc drive (**C:**) icon to display the folders. Find the files and folders you want to copy to the CD and highlight them. Select **Copy this folder** (or **file** or **selected items**, whichever appears) from the **File and Folder Tasks** menu on the left of the window as shown below.

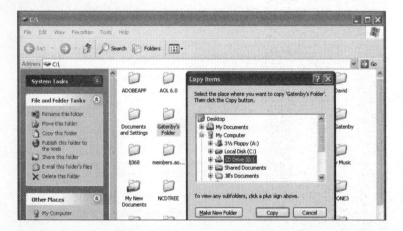

Next select **CD Drive (D:)** from the **Copy Items** window shown above and then click the **Copy** button.

The files to be copied to the CD are first copied to an image file on your hard disc, prior to copying to the CD. A new window should appear with the files listed under the heading **Files Ready to be Written to the CD** as shown below.

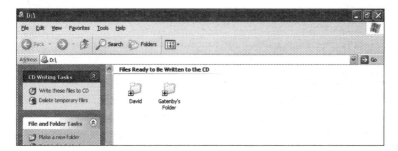

Highlight the files and select **Write these files to CD** from the **CD Writing Tasks** menu shown on the left-hand side above. This starts the **CD Writing Wizard**, where you are able to give a name to the CD if you don't want to use the default name supplied.

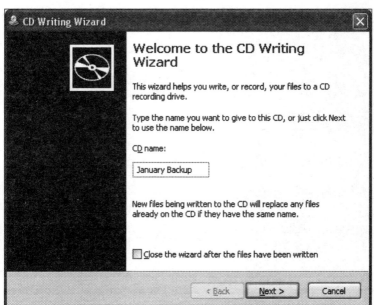

After clicking **Next** a window appears showing the progress being made in the copying process.

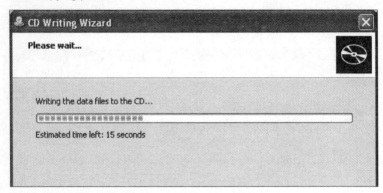

All being well the copying process will be successful and you will see the following window, which also gives you the opportunity to copy the same set of files to another CD.

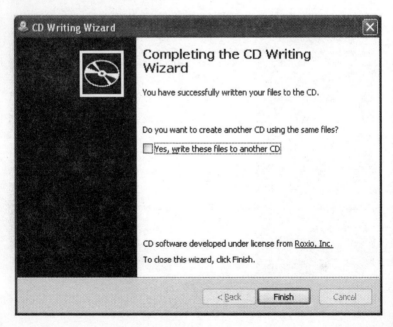

Using Nero to Create a Data CD

The Creative Blaster CD-RW drive uses the well-known Nero software for the task of burning a CD-R. The Nero software can also be bought separately for use with other brands of CD-RW drives. Selecting **Nero-Burning ROM** from the **start** and **All Programs** menu leads to the **Nero Wizard**. This guides you through the process of supplying Nero with your CD burning requirements such as **Data CD** or **Audio CD** or other formats.

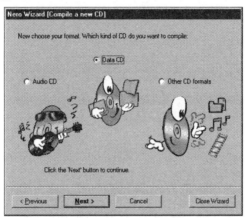

Then you select the files and folders you wish to copy to the CD-R using the windows of Nero's Explorer-like interface. The required folders are then dragged and dropped onto the CD named **NEW** as shown below.

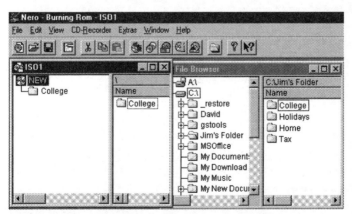

Finally the Nero Wizard gives you the chance to **Test**, **Test and burn** or simply **Burn** the CD.

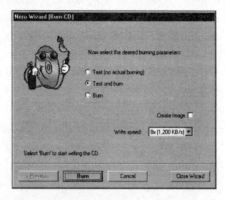

You are informed of progress while the CD is burned and when the burn process has been successfully completed.

Both CD-R and CD-RW are very suitable as backup media. One of their main advantages is the low price of the media. In particular the CD-R discs are now so cheap that you can afford to treat them as disposables for distributing files to colleagues or for backing up important files. The CD also has a greater capacity (nominally 650MB) compared with the floppy disc (1.44MB) or the ZIP disc (100 or 250MB). Using writeable CDs for backup and emergency recovery is discussed in more detail later in this book.

I have used Nero to make regular backups of my work onto CD-R. Nero has also been used to make copies of entire books onto CD (in Adobe Acrobat format). These are posted to the commercial printers to enable printing direct from CD. The Nero software has always been very fast and reliable in my experience.

Backing Up to a Second Hard Disc Drive

If your computer has a second hard disc drive with plenty of free space, it makes sense to use it to make quick backup copies of important work. This is not a completely secure backup system as it does not give protection against some of the major causes of data loss. For example, if the computer is stolen or damaged in a fire or flood, you will still lose the data and programs.

However, if you have already fitted a new hard disc drive (discussed later in this book) it may be worth keeping the old hard disc drive installed as a backup device. This is very convenient for making quick backup copies, which will at least give protection against accidental deletion of files or damage to your main hard disc. In addition, it is essential that you also make regular secure backups on a separate medium such as a ZIP disc, CD or tape cartridge.

A strategy which served me well in producing numerous books over several years is as follows: Save the work on the main hard disc (the **C:** drive) every few minutes by clicking on the disc icon on the Toolbar, shown left. Backups to the second hard drive (drive **F:**) are made less frequently, perhaps every hour. Secure backups are made to a ZIP drive and writeable CD every day.

While you are working on a word processing task, for example, simply select **File** and **Save As...**. Then select the second drive (perhaps the **E:** or **F:** drive) and make an extra copy. Before saving on the **C:** drive again the **C:** drive will need to be reselected using **Save As...**.

Alternatively you can use the Windows Explorer to drag and drop a file onto the second hard disc. To use drag and drop, you must make sure the file is not open in its associated program. For example, to copy a Word file, the file to be copied must not be open in the Word program.

Tape Backup Systems

Earlier notes described the copying of files and folders using "drag and drop" in the Windows Explorer. This is quite efficient for copying relatively small sets of files and folders. However, in a business or professional situation it is prudent to make regular backups of the *entire* hard disc contents. With modern PCs having hard discs of typically 20 or 40GB or more capacity, the floppy disc, ZIP disc and CD just do not have the necessary capacity. Even a second high capacity hard disc is not a secure solution since this is vulnerable to fire, theft, etc.

In a business or college with a network, for example, the work of hundreds of people may be stored on the hard disc of one central computer, known as the *file server*. A single backup operation is needed which can back up everyone's work and all of the system software on one high capacity storage medium.

For the systematic, regular backups of the entire hard disc, a tape backup system is a popular solution. Systems like the HP Colorado tape drive, using *tape cartridges* of typically 14GB or 20GB, enable all of the system software and applications (programs) and all of the data files (your work) to be backed up.

For commercial applications, data cartridges with a storage capacity of 200GB are available. In a business situation where security is crucial, backup tape cartridges should be stored in a different building from the computers holding the original files, to guard against damage from fire or floods, etc.

The complete tape backup package includes the tape drive and the backup software. There is usually a choice of internal or external tape drives. The internal drive obviously provides a neater and more compact solution; the external drive is portable, enabling you to transfer a backup to another computer, if necessary.

A full backup including both programs and data is essential to restore the system if the entire hard disc fails, or is severely damaged or stolen. Making a full tape backup is a lengthy process, taking a few hours to copy a large hard disc. It is important to check before buying any tape backup system that it can accommodate a full backup of your entire hard disc on a single cartridge. If a single tape cannot accommodate the full backup, the process will be halted and the computer will "sit" waiting, usually overnight, for another tape to be inserted.

This defeats the object of the automated backup, which should proceed unattended, at a time when the computer is not being used. Special backup software (discussed shortly) includes many special features such as the ability to schedule unattended backups. In a business situation this is essential, since tape backups are relatively slow, taking hours rather than minutes. It's therefore common to schedule an unattended backup to take place in the middle of the night, when the computer would not normally be used.

The Full Backup

The full backup (of an entire hard disc) is essential if you are to recover from a major disaster. This backup includes not only your important data files representing hours of toil, but also the program files like the Windows XP operating system and applications like Microsoft Office

Features of backup Software

Some of the features of dedicated backup software are:

- Full backups of an entire drive.
- Selection sets of files which are backed up on a regular basis.
- Scheduling of backups at specified times.
- Back up to various media such as floppy disc, CD or tape cartridge.
- Error checking (verification) to ensure the backup is accurate.
- File compression to maximise storage space.
- Incremental backups which only back up files that have changed (since the last backup).
- *Restoration* to the original location or a specified location on the hard disc.

Fitting an Internal Tape Drive

You don't need any special tools to fit a tape drive - just a small screwdriver. This is a task which anyone can do - you don't need any technical or electronic expertise. A brief outline of the installation process is as follows:

- Make sure the computer is switched off before touching or working on any components.

- Rid yourself of static electricity by frequently touching the metal case of the computer. Alternatively use a special earthing strap obtainable from any electrical components shop.

- Take the cover off the computer and remove one of the blanking plates covering a vacant "bay" at the front of the machine.

- Slide the tape drive into the vacant bay in the casing and secure at the sides with the small screws which should be provided with the tape drive.

- Connect the tape drive to the floppy drive controller (a slot on the computer "motherboard") using a data cable. (This is a wide, flat, ribbon cable with a coloured stripe down one edge). You can either use the existing floppy drive data cable or use the new ribbon cable normally provided with the tape drive. Refer to the tape drive installation guide - the position of the coloured stripe is critical.

- There should be at least one spare set of brightly coloured power leads terminating in a white connecting plug. Carefully plug a set of power leads into the back of the tape drive.

- Replace the computer casing and switch on.

- After fitting a tape unit, your computer should automatically detect the new tape drive on startup and find and install the necessary software from the Windows XP CD, or from the discs provided in the drive package.

Some packages include a diagnostic program which performs a large number of write operations to test that the system can record properly.

Restoring Files from Tape to Hard Disc

Tape drives are relatively slow devices, so restoration of a large backup from tape can take several hours. The destination of the restored files may be their original location on the hard disc, i.e. the files are restored to the same folder in which they were originally created. Alternatively it's possible to restore files to an entirely new folder, perhaps on a different hard disc drive.

Developing a Backup Strategy

If you regularly back up all of the files in a particular backup job (either a full backup or selected files backup), you will be repeatedly copying and overwriting files which haven't changed. To avoid this, first make a full backup of all of the files. Subsequently you back up only those files which have recently changed. Then if you need to restore your hard disc you use the full backup together with the backup(s) of the changed files.

The Archive Bit

This is a property or attribute of all files and acts like a flag. When a file is created or modified, the archive bit is switched on. This indicates that a file needs to be backed up. The archive bit can be viewed by selecting the file in Windows Explorer then clicking **File** and **Properties**.

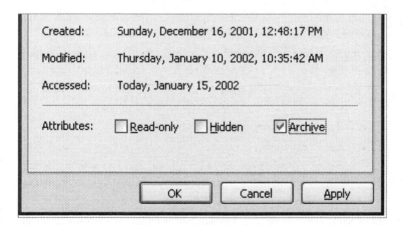

Differential and Incremental Backups

These two options in backup programs examine the archive attribute and back up only files which have changed. They produce different backup sets because of the way they handle the archive bit.

Differential Backup

This backs up all files that have changed at any time since the last *full* backup. After a differential backup the archive bit remains on. To restore a backup you only need the full backup plus the latest differential backup.

Incremental Backup

This backs up all the files that have changed since the last *incremental* backup. After an incremental backup of a file the archive attribute is switched off.

The incremental backup should therefore be quicker than the differential backup but is more complicated to restore. Restoring an incremental backup requires the last full backup plus all of the subsequent incremental backups.

The purpose of using the differential and incremental backups rather than full backups is to save time spent unnecessarily copying files when perfectly good backup copies already exist on tape. The cost of managing a backup system should be appropriate to the value of the data. However, an organization with a cavalier attitude to backup systems may find its very survival is threatened in the case of a hard disc failure.

How Many Backup Tapes?

Even with a tape backup system capable of copying the entire contents of the hard disc, it's still possible for disaster to strike unless a reliable backup strategy is devised. Below are some possible scenarios which could lead to a crisis; they can be avoided with a little planning.

- You only have a single tape and you overwrite it with each new backup. There is a problem during the backup, causing the data on both the hard disc and the tape to be corrupted.

  Your data is lost for ever and the data files must be re-created from scratch, by retyping all of the data.

- You only back up once a week and the hard disc fails just before the backup is due.

  The best part of a week's work could be lost.

- You do a daily full backup with a separate tape for each day, but there is a serious problem (possibly caused by a virus) which goes undetected for over a week.

  All of the backup tapes would be damaged.

The safest solution is to have a lot of backup tapes covering as long a time span as possible. However, backup tapes are expensive and the time to manage the backup process must also be considered.

A simple but expensive solution would be to have a separate backup tape for each day of the week and to make a daily full backup. Then have two or three similar sets of tapes, each covering a week's backups, to be used in rotation. This would help to overcome most of the problems listed above.

You could use fewer tapes by making incremental backups on certain days, including only *modified* files. The incremental backups could be made with the *append* option set so that they all fit on one tape. A suggestion for a possible backup strategy is given on the next page.

A Possible Backup Strategy

1. Dedicate one tape to a weekly full backup. Use another tape for the remaining days of the week to hold all of the daily incremental backups.

2. Repeat the process the following week, but using a different set of tapes.

3. Complete a three week cycle with a third set of tapes.

4. In the fourth week, return to the first set of tapes and overwrite them. Continue to rotate the tapes in a three week cycle.

Summary: Backup Activities

*   The contents of your hard disc, including both software and data files, represents a huge investment of time and money, often exceeding the value of the computer itself.

*   The main reason for backing up files is to enable a recovery of the contents of your hard disc, which are vulnerable to damage or loss.

*   Without an adequate backup system, loss of the hard disc contents can be a catastrophe, because of the time and costs involved in restoring the software and data files.

*   A secondary reason for backups is to transfer files between computers; for example, between work and home.

*   Archiving is the copying of files which are seldom used, onto a disc or tape, in order to save hard disc space. The archived files can be retrieved later, if necessary.

*   Full system backups copy the entire contents of the hard disc onto a tape cartridge. The tape has a capacity equivalent to several thousand floppy discs.

*   In a partial backup, small selections of files can be backed up onto floppy discs, ZIP discs, writeable CD or tape. Programs like WinZip allow files to be compressed, effectively increasing the capacity of the backup medium.

- Backup discs and tapes should be stored in a secure place well away from the room where the computer is located.

- Removable Hard Discs, such as the ZIP and Jaz discs, can perform a valuable role as a fast backup medium for large groups of data files and software. The Iomega ZIP drive has its own powerful tools to facilitate the copying of files and discs.

- The external ZIP drive is portable and can easily be connected to other computers for the transfer of data files and software. The system is much faster and has far greater capacity than the floppy disc.

- A second hard disc drive is not a complete backup solution, but provides a fast method of duplicating files, giving protection against some eventualities.

- The writeable Compact Disc (CD-R and CD-RW) is a very cheap, fast and reliable backup medium capable of storing substantial amounts of data. CD-R discs can only be written to once. CD-RW discs can be written to many times and can be used for drag and drop copying like a floppy or ZIP disc.

- Windows XP introduces its own CD burning software based on the popular Easy CD Creator from Roxio Inc. A greater range of features can be obtained by upgrading to the full Easy CD Creator Platinum version. Nero from Ahead Software is another well-established CD burning package.

- Files can be restored to the original folder or to a specified folder, perhaps on a different hard disc.

- You can restore all of the files from a backup or just a small selection of files from within the backup.

- It's a good idea, after a backup, to do a test restoration of a few sample files, to check that the backup and restoration are working correctly.

The next chapter describes the main features of the backup software provided as a component of Windows XP.

4   Backup Activities

Windows XP Backup

Introduction

Limited copying of files and directories can be carried out using "drag and drop" in the Windows Explorer or My Computer, etc., as described previously. This is quite efficient for copying small sets of files and directories onto removable media on an occasional basis. However, for the systematic, regular backups of larger files or for backing up the entire hard disc, dedicated backup software is necessary which automates the process and provides a lot of additional facilities. Some of the features of dedicated backup software are as follows.

- Full backups of an entire drive.

- Selection sets of files which are backed up on a regular basis.

- Scheduling of backups at specified times.

- Back up to various media such as floppy disc, ZIP/Jaz discs, CD-R, CD-RW and tape. Disc spanning if necessary.

- Error checking (verification) to ensure the backup is accurate.

- File compression to maximise storage space.

- Differential and Incremental backups which only back up files that have changed (since the last backup).

- Restoration to the original location or a specified location on the hard disc.

Windows XP Professional includes a fully featured backup program. This is not included in Windows XP Home Edition. However, the Veritas Backup Exec Desktop software is a very close relative of the Windows XP backup program and is available separately, for a modest price.

The backup process can be started by selecting **start**, **All Programs**, **Accessories**, **System Tools** and **Backup**. Alternatively you can click **start** and **Control Panel** and **Performance and Maintenance** then select **Back up your data** as shown below.

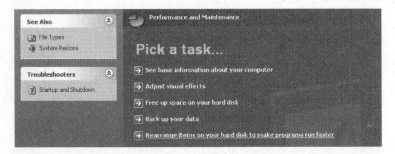

The **Backup or Restore Wizard** welcome screen opens and there is an option for experienced users to select **Advanced Mode** where settings can be changed. Most users will probably prefer to use the wizard initially and the next screen asks you to choose between either backing up or restoring files. (A restore operation copies a previous backup from a removable backup medium to a hard disc). You are then asked to select what you want to back up, such as everything on the computer or files that you select.

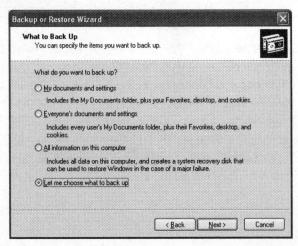

If you select **Let me choose what to back up** from the previous window the wizard presents an Explorer-like interface. Double clicking **My Computer** in the left-hand panel allows you to display the contents of your hard disc and select (with a tick) the files and/or folders to be included in the backup, as shown below.

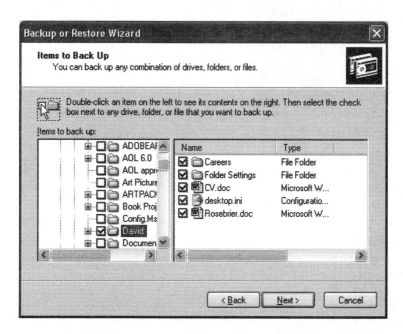

After clicking **Next** you are presented with a window to select the destination for the backup (floppy disc, ZIP disc, tape cartridge or CD, etc.) You can also enter the name for the backup to identify it on the backup medium. The wizard then presents a screen summarizing the details of the backup. If you click the **Advanced...** button the wizard continues with a number of further options such as the type of backup, appending or replacing existing backups and scheduling a backup to take place at a particular time. These advanced options are discussed shortly.

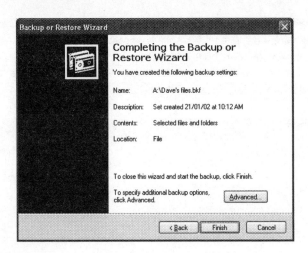

When you click **Finish** on the **Completing the Backup or Restore Wizard** screen, the copying of files starts and you are informed of progress throughout the backup. If the backup needs to span more than one disc or tape you will be prompted to insert another.

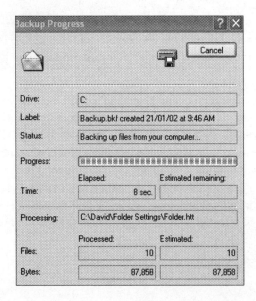

On completion of the backup the progress screen includes a **Report** button allowing you to see a log file listing full details and any errors which occurred during the backup process.

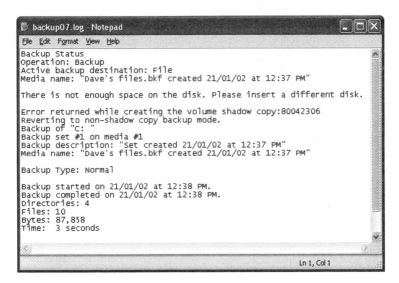

```
backup07.log - Notepad
File  Edit  Format  View  Help
Backup Status
Operation: Backup
Active backup destination: File
Media name: "Dave's files.bkf created 21/01/02 at 12:37 PM"

There is not enough space on the disk. Please insert a different disk.

Error returned while creating the volume shadow copy:80042306
Reverting to non-shadow copy backup mode.
Backup of "C: "
Backup set #1 on media #1
Backup description: "Set created 21/01/02 at 12:37 PM"
Media name: "Dave's files.bkf created 21/01/02 at 12:37 PM"

Backup Type: Normal

Backup started on 21/01/02 at 12:38 PM.
Backup completed on 21/01/02 at 12:38 PM.
Directories: 4
Files: 10
Bytes: 87,858
Time:  3 seconds
                                                              Ln 1, Col 1
```

Please note that for the purposes of this example I have only backed up a few files onto a floppy disc. A realistic backup would involve much more data and take a lot longer..

Advanced Mode

More experienced users may wish to specify more of their own settings than is possible using the Backup or Restore Wizard. This can be achieved by selecting **Advanced Mode** from the welcome screen at the beginning of the wizard.

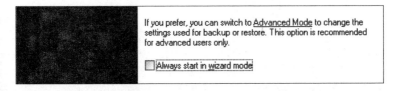

If you prefer, you can switch to <u>Advanced Mode</u> to change the settings used for backup or restore. This option is recommended for advanced users only.

☐ Always start in wizard mode

The welcome screen for **Advanced Mode** appears, as shown below.

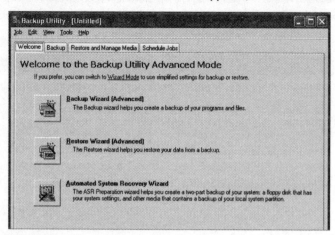

As well as advanced versions of the Backup and Restore Wizards there is the **Automated System Recovery Wizard** which allows you to back up important system files and create a recovery (floppy) disc.

If you select the **Backup** tab as shown above, you are presented with the main backup window shown below. This enables you to specify all of the main backup settings from a single screen.

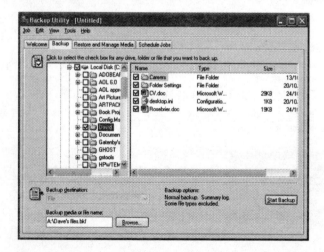

On the window shown previously files to be backed up are highlighted in an Explorer-like interface. The hierarchy of discs and folders is shown in the left-hand panel and individual files and folders can be selected by ticking in the right-hand panel. You can set the destination for the backup (such as floppy disc, ZIP disc, tape or CD, etc.) using the **Backup media or file name** bar at the bottom of the window.

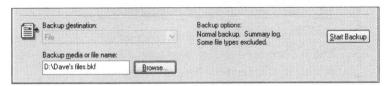

Further options can be obtained by selecting **Tools** and **Options...** from the menu bar in the main backup window, as shown at the bottom of the previous page. The **Backup Type** tab in the resulting **Options** window includes various types of backup such as differential and incremental, as discussed in the previous chapter.

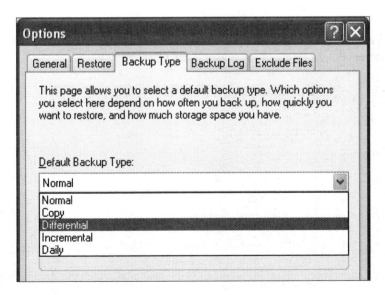

- A **Normal** backup copies all of the selected files and modifies the archive bit (discussed in the last chapter) to indicate that they have been backed up.

- The **Copy** backup copies selected files but does not mark them as backed up.

- The **Differential** backup only backs up files that have been created or changed since the last normal backup.

- The **Incremental** backup only copies files that have been created or changed since the last incremental backup.

- The **Daily** backup copies the files that have been created or modified on the day of the backup.

When you have completed the settings for the backup click the **Start Backup** button on the main window shown at the top of the previous page. A window appears giving details of the backup you have set up. There is a choice between overwriting any existing files on the backup media or appending the new files to the end of previous backups.

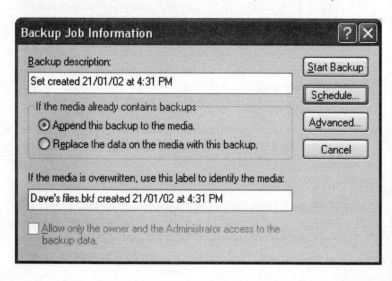

The **Schedule** button shown in the previous window allows you to start the backup automatically at a convenient time. In many businesses backups are scheduled to take place in the middle of the night when no-one is using the computers. A name must be given to the scheduled backup job as shown below.

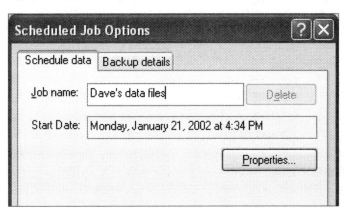

The **Advanced...** button on the previous **Backup Job Information** window enables you to verify the data after backup. Verification checks for errors in the backup by comparing the files recorded on the backup medium with those in their original location on the hard disc.

Keeping the Backups Safe

At this point, your backup should now be safely stored on one or more removable backup discs or tapes. The backup can *span* several media if necessary. The backup media should be clearly labelled and locked away in a different physical location from your computer, to guard against the risk of a disaster such as fire, theft or flooding.

The Restoration Process

Restoration is the process of copying files from the backup disc or tape, back onto the original hard disc or onto a different hard disc. The entire backup set of files may be restored or, alternatively, it's possible to restore just a small selection of files. Although we hope backups will never need to be restored in a crisis, it makes sense to find out how to do the job beforehand. As a practice exercise, you don't need to restore the entire backup, just select one or two files to make sure everything is working correctly.

Restoring a Backup

You will need your backup media (floppy discs, ZIP discs, CDs or tapes, etc.) at hand. Insert the backup media. The restore process is started by selecting **start**, **All Programs**, **Accessories**, **System Tools** and **Backup**. Alternatively you can click **start** and **Control Panel** and **Performance and Maintenance** then select **Back up your data**. From the **Backup or Restore Wizard** click **Next** on the welcome screen then select **Restore files and settings**. The next window displays an Explorer-like interface which allows you to select what is to be restored - either the whole backup or a selection of files and/or folders.

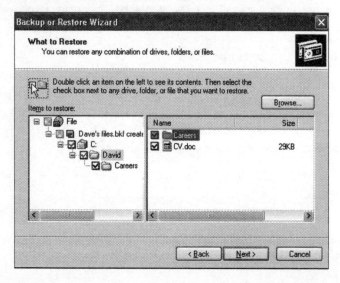

When you have selected the required files and/or folders to restore, by placing ticks in the adjacent check boxes, click **Next** and you are presented with a window summarising the restore settings, as shown below.

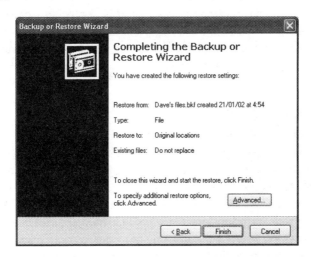

Note in the above window that, by default, the files are restored to their original location on the hard disc. If you wish to restore the files to a different location (from whence they were copied in the backup) click the **Advanced**... button and you are given the opportunity to specify an **Alternate location** in which to save the restored files on the hard disc.

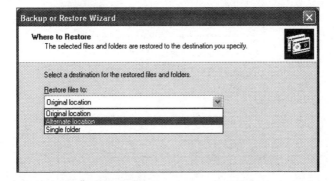

Please also note that by default when files are restored to their original locations, existing files of the same name are not replaced. This is shown in the upper screenshot on the previous page. However, if you have chosen to select **Advanced…** as discussed on the previous page, then you are given the chance to specify how to restore the files.

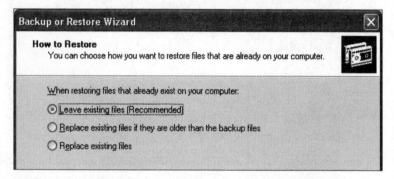

If files already exist of the same name, they can either be left in place or they can be replaced by the files from the backup. The second option only replaces the existing files if they are older than the files from the backup media.

When you click **Finish** the restore operation begins and you are informed of progress throughout and at the end.

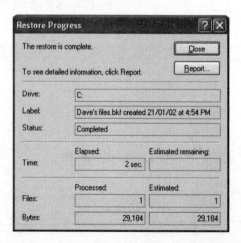

A report on the restore process can be displayed by clicking the **Report...** button on the final **Restore Progress** window shown previously.

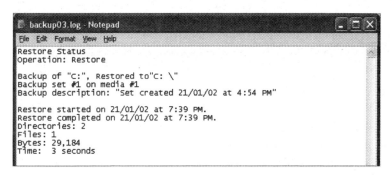

Please note that for advanced users the restore process can be controlled from a single window as shown below. This is launched by selecting **Advanced Mode** from the welcome screen of the **Backup or Restore Wizard** then clicking the **Restore and Manage Media** tab.

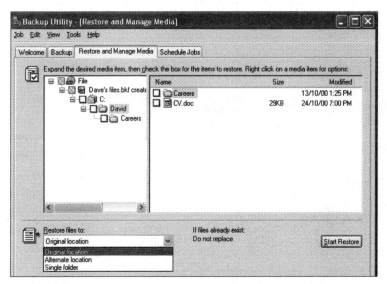

Summary: Windows XP Backup

- The backup software in Windows XP is a fully-featured backup program based on the well-established VERITAS Backup software. The backup software is not available in Windows XP Home Edition but may be purchased separately.

- The program can be operated most easily using the Backup or Restore Wizard which guides you through the setup process in a series of windows. More advanced users can use a single window to specify their own backup settings.

- Backup software allows you to copy to floppy disc, ZIP/Jaz disc, CD-R and CD-RW and tape cartridge. (Backups to another hard disc within the computer are not secure backups since they do not give protection against theft or fire, etc.)

- A backup can include all selected files or only those files that have changed since the last backup.

- Windows XP allows long filenames; backups can be given meaningful names which help in the identification and efficient management of backups.

- The *compare* or *verify* option checks that the files on the backup medium are an exact copy of the original files on the hard disc.

- Files can be restored to the original folder or to a specified folder, perhaps on a different hard disc.

- It's a good idea, after a backup, to do a test restoration of a few sample files, to check that the backup and restoration are working correctly and that you are familiar with the process.

- Backup media should be stored in a location which is secure and away from the computer containing the original files. This should guard against the loss of the data after disasters such as fire or flooding.

Protection Against Viruses

Introduction - What is a Virus?

A virus is a small computer program written maliciously to cause damage to software and data and to cause inconvenience to the user. The virus enters a computer system insidiously, often from a rogue floppy disc or an e-mail. If not detected the virus replicates and spreads throughout a hard disc; some viruses may only cause trivial damage - such as displaying a so-called 'humorous' message - while others can destroy files or wipe an entire hard disc.

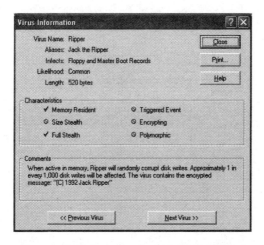

Even when a virus doesn't do any serious damage to files and software, the time spent in eradicating it is likely to be considerable - not to mention the anxiety caused to the user whose work is interrupted, possibly for a long time.

Writing viruses is an act of vandalism and can result in a prison sentence. Virus writers are invariably male, presumably seeing the virus as a demonstration of their misplaced skill.

Viruses can exist on floppy and hard discs. They can also reside temporarily in the computer's memory - but they are removed from the memory when the computer is switched off. Viruses do not permanently damage the physical parts of a computer - hardware components such as the memory or the printer.

Floppy discs are a major source of virus infection, but viruses can also enter your system via a modem from the Internet, perhaps through e-mail *attachments*, the programs or documents "clipped" onto an e-mail.

The Norton AntiVirus 2002 software package has a scanning program (**Auto-Protect**) which constantly monitors e-mail attachments being downloaded to your computer from an Internet mail server.

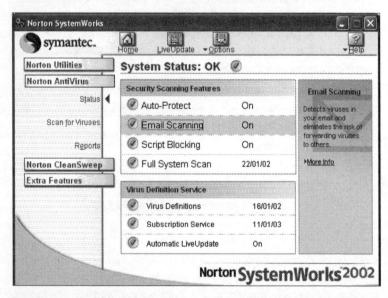

Great care should be taken when opening e-mails of doubtful origin; if you are suspicious the e-mail should be deleted immediately without opening the attachments.

Types of Virus

The File Virus

File viruses attach themselves to *program* or *executable* files. These files (having extensions such as .EXE, .COM, .SYS, etc.) are part of applications software packages like Microsoft Word or Excel. The file virus (also known as the *program* virus) does not infect the *documents* produced using the software, although documents can be infected by the macro virus discussed next. (In this context, the term *document* includes not only text produced in a word processor but other types of file saved on disc, such as Excel spreadsheets.)

The Macro Virus

This type of virus has been developed to infect the *documents* produced using programs such as Word and Excel. These documents have their own inbuilt programming language. This allows the advanced user to write *macros*, or small routines for automating frequently used groups of instructions. Unfortunately the virus writers have found ways of writing viruses in the macro language. Now even Word documents and Excel spreadsheets are vulnerable to virus attack.

So it's possible for your hard disc to be infected with viruses spread in document files received via the Internet as attachments to e-mail (as well as files transferred from floppy disc).

Boot Sector Viruses

The boot sector is an area of a floppy or hard disc and contains information needed when the computer is started up or "booted".

Even a floppy disc containing only data files (rather than programs) has a boot sector which can be infected by a virus. If such an infected floppy disc is inadvertently left in a disc drive when the computer is switched off, next time the machine is "booted up" (i.e. started), the virus can spread via the memory to the hard disc, where it can wreak havoc.

Stealth Viruses

There are many ways in which the virus writer tries to cause damage whilst avoiding detection. The stealth virus actively tries to conceal itself by making the computer behave normally until it's ready to strike.

Trojans

The Trojan, as its name implies, is a program with an apparently genuine function, but which is really designed to do damage. It is not a virus since it does not replicate itself.

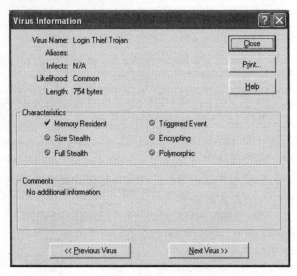

One such Trojan takes over a user's e-mail and uses it to send offensive messages - damaging the reputation of the innocent user. Logic Bombs and Time Bombs are types of Trojan which are triggered when a certain event or date occurs such as Friday 13th. The Michelangelo virus is triggered on the painter's birthday, March 6th.

The Polymorphic Virus

This changes its identity every time it replicates; it does this by repeatedly encrypting or encoding itself.

At the time of writing there are over 58,000 known viruses, as listed in the Virus List provided with Norton AntiVirus. Hundreds of new viruses are discovered every month. The names are assigned by the anti-virus firms or by the virus writers themselves. Each of these known viruses consists of a unique piece of programming code which the main anti-virus packages can detect. This code is known as the virus "signature".

Another common problem is the hoax e-mail, warning of the dangers of a non-existent virus. Although harmless in that no damage is caused to the computer or its software, the effect is to spread panic and anxiety amongst a large number of people.

Requirements of Anti-Virus Software

The last ten years have seen the evolution of an ever-increasing list of computer viruses. Windows XP does not contain its own anti-virus software. However, several major companies have developed anti-virus software to detect and eradicate virus infection. Three of the leading software packages are Norton AntiVirus 2002, McAfee VirusScan, and Dr. Solomon's Anti-Virus Toolkit. These provide users with regular updates of virus definitions. Then the latest viruses can be detected and dealt with. Methods of dealing with viruses are discussed shortly.

The anti-virus software must find and destroy the existing base of many thousands of known viruses. A small extract from the **Virus List** from Norton AntiVirus 2002 is shown on the right. The anti-virus software must also recognize any 'virus-like activity,' possibly caused by new and unknown viruses.

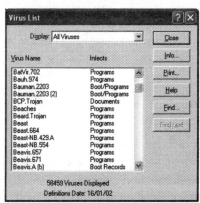

Virus-like activity would include the computer trying to alter program files - this shouldn't happen during the normal operation of the computer.

Some of main functions of anti-virus software are therefore:

- To continually monitor the memory and vulnerable files, to prevent viruses entering the hard disc and spreading, causing havoc and destruction. The **Auto-Protect** feature in Norton AntiVirus is a *memory resident* program which is always running in the background.

- To allow the user to carry out *manual scans* to check the memory, floppy and hard discs, whenever it is felt necessary.

- To remove viruses by repairing or deleting infected files.

- To provide a list of definitions of known viruses, which is regularly updated and distributed to the user, perhaps via the Internet.

It is also possible to *schedule* regular scans at certain times on particular days of the week.

The complete anti-virus software is permanently installed on the hard disc from where a manual scan can be run from the **Programs** menu.

In addition, should the hard disc become severely infected, a "bootable" floppy disc or CD containing the main virus repair program should be available. If a virus strikes, the computer should be shut down to stop the virus spreading. Then the computer can be started from the "rescue" or emergency disc and the virus removed from the hard disc.

Features of Anti-Virus Software

When you buy a complete anti-virus package such as Norton AntiVirus 2002, McAfee VirusScan, or Dr. Solomon's Anti-Virus Toolkit, the package will usually comprise a suite of programs providing two different modes of scanning:

First, a scan available "on demand" from the Windows XP menus, like any other piece of software. This is often referred to as a Manual Scan.

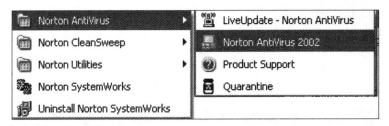

Secondly, a virus scanner which starts up automatically and runs continually in the background, checking files before they are used or as they are received from the e-mail server. Norton AntiVirus 2002 runs the **Auto-Protect** feature from the time Windows XP starts up.

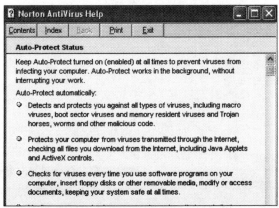

Anti-virus scanners which run continually may need to be temporarily disabled (but not uninstalled) while new software is installed. To temporarily disable the **Auto-Protect** feature in **Norton AntiVirus 2002**, you right click over its icon on the Windows XP taskbar.

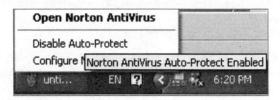

When you are ready to switch the auto scanner back on, invoke the above menu again. This will have changed to display the option **Enable Auto-Protect**.

The Manual Scan

This is the main scanning program launched from the Windows XP program menu. The user can select this scan whenever they wish to check the hard disc or a newly acquired floppy disc. This scanner also carries out the repair of files containing viruses.

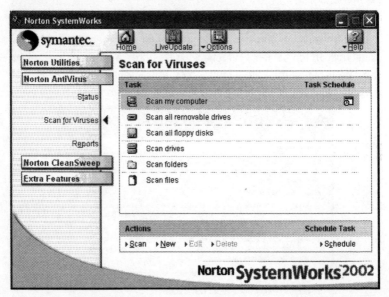

If you select the **Options** button shown in the previous window and then click **Norton AntiVirus,** you are presented with the dialogue box shown below. There are different options listed on the right, depending on which **System** is selected in the left-hand panel, e.g. **Auto-Protect** or **Manual Scan**. You can choose when to start **Auto-Protect** and to switch on or off the scanning of e-mail. **Comprehensive file scanning** checks every file on your hard disc.

Scan files using SmartScan examines only those files most likely to be infected by viruses, according to a list of file types. This is the **Program File Extension** list, which can be altered after clicking the **Customize** button. Norton AntiVirus 2002 can also check *compressed files*. Files are not normally infected in their compressed state, but a compressed file might contain a virus which was contracted before it was compressed. You can also select how the program is to respond if a virus is found.

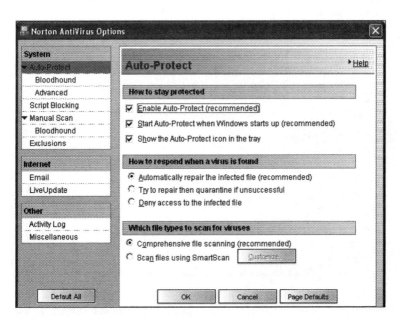

In the previous dialogue box, **Quarantine** in Norton AntiVirus 2002 refers to a method of isolating unknown viruses which can't be removed with the existing list of virus definitions. Once in the Quarantine, the virus can't infect the files on the hard disc.

Viruses in the Quarantine area can be sent over the Internet to the Symantec AntiVirus Research Center where they can be examined. If a new virus is discovered it can be added to the list of virus definitions. This can be downloaded by other Norton AntiVirus 2002 users next time they update their list of virus definitions.

Bloodhound listed in the left-hand panel of the previous window is the name of a feature designed to detect new and unknown viruses.

The Scanning Process

Once the scan is underway you are informed of progress as shown below.

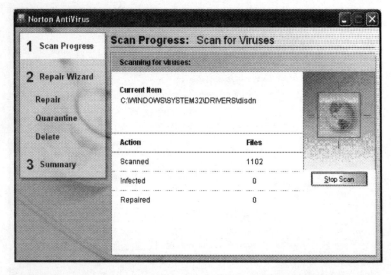

During the scan, viruses which are known can be detected by their "signature" - a unique set of program code or lines of instructions. In the case of new, unknown viruses, the anti-virus software looks for "virus-like activity".

If a virus attaches itself to a program, the size of the program file will increase, not something you'd expect in normal usage. However, the stealth virus, for example, tries to avoid detection by falsifying the file size entry, so that the file appears not to have changed.

If a Virus Strikes

If you are unfortunate enough to suffer a virus infection, a warning message will appear on the screen, possibly accompanied by an alarm sound. On finding a virus, the anti-virus programs will prevent access to the infected file.

Normally the software will try to "clean" the infected file by removing the illicit lines of code which constitute the virus. Otherwise the file must be deleted or excluded. Alternatively the program can be set up to take a specific action if a virus is found, as shown below.

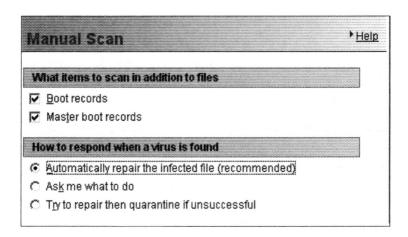

If Norton Antivirus is unable to repair or quarantine an infected file, the file is deleted.

The Virus in Memory

This is an extremely dangerous situation, since the virus is ideally placed to damage any files which are run or accessed from hard or floppy disc.

If you suspect there may be a virus in memory:

* Shut down the computer immediately, using the correct procedure.

* Switch off the power to the computer. (This will remove the virus from memory).

* Re-start the computer using a special anti-virus floppy boot disc or CD (These must be known to be free from viruses.) Floppy discs should be write-protected in this situation.

The main anti-virus packages include a disc or CD version of the virus detection/repair program. Use this emergency disc to start the computer and to find and repair any suspected viruses on the hard disc.

In Norton AntiVirus, if you shut your computer down because of a suspected virus, or if it won't start because of a boot sector virus, you can use the Norton CD as an emergency disc. This should allow you to start the computer, carry out a full virus scan and remove the viruses.

Changing the Boot Sequence of Your Computer

You may need to alter the startup sequence of your computer to enable it to "boot up" from a CD or floppy disc.

This involves changing the startup options in a special section of memory known as the *CMOS RAM*. The CMOS memory contains many crucial settings for your computer and is powered by a battery so that the settings are not lost when the computer is switched off.

To change the CMOS settings, you need to enter the **SETUP** program of your computer. Soon after switching the computer on, watch for a message such as:

"Press DEL if you want to run SETUP"

On entering the setup program, you will probably need to highlight a line like:

Advanced CMOS setup

After pressing the **Enter** or **Return** key, look for a line like:

1st Boot Device: IDE-0

To boot from a removable disc such as a CD or floppy disc this line needs to be altered to something like:

1st Boot Device: CDROM

or   **1st Boot Device: FLOPPY**

If you need to change a CMOS setting, a common method is to highlight the setting and then press **Page Up** or **Page Down** to cycle through the various alternatives. Follow the instructions on the screen to save the new settings and then leave the CMOS setup program.

The computer should now boot up from the emergency CD or floppy disc. Follow the instructions on the screen to detect and remove any viruses. On completion you will need to restart the computer, enter the BIOS/CMOS as before and restore the original boot device line, such as:

Ist Boot Device: IDE-0

Save the settings, usually by pressing the **Escape** key and then selecting:

Save Settings and Exit

If you now press **Enter** or **Return** the computer should continue with the startup process, booting from the hard disc as normal and fully restored to health.

Infected Floppy Discs

If it is suspected that a large number of floppy discs may be infected, they must all be scanned and any viruses dealt with by repair or deletion. In a large organisation, such as a school or college where hundreds of students may back up their work onto floppy disc, this could be a massive task requiring the allocation of considerable time.

Updating Your Virus Definitions

Since new viruses are discovered constantly, you are advised to update your virus definition list at regular intervals, weekly say. Some anti-virus software companies send out updates on floppy disc. Norton AntiVirus allows your virus list to be updated automatically when you connect to the Internet or when you select a **LiveUpdate** from the main window.

After connecting to the Internet **LiveUpdate** checks to see if you need any downloads to bring your system up to date.

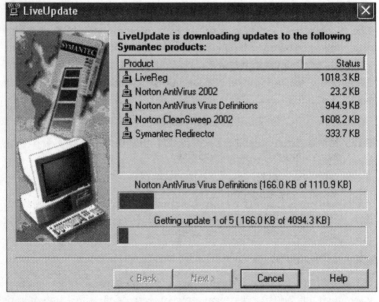

As the list in the above window shows, apart from AntiVirus 2002, any other Norton products installed on your computer, are also checked and updated if necessary. At the end of the process you are informed of the components of your system that now contain the latest information.

Summary: Protection Against Viruses

- Obtain an established anti-virus package such as Norton AntiVirus 2002, McAfee VirusScan, or Dr. Solomon's Anti-Virus Toolkit.

- Install the anti-virus software on your hard disc, configured to provide scans:

    1   automatically on startup and continually in the background while the computer is running

    2   manually i.e. selected from the menus on demand

    3   at regular times, scheduled automatically

- Obtain and install regular software upgrades so that the virus definition list is always up-to-date with the latest known viruses.

- Always run a manual check on all floppy discs acquired from elsewhere. Be extremely sceptical about all discs - even brand new packaged software from reputable companies has been known to be infected.

- If you distribute files yourself, either on floppy disc, ZIP disc, CD or via the Internet, make sure they are scanned and virus free. Although organizations should scan all incoming files and discs, it is better to safeguard your own interests by scanning everything before you send it out.

- Carry out regular (weekly, say) manual or scheduled checks on all hard and floppy discs.

- Be vigilant when other people use the computer - insist that any removable discs are scanned before use.

- Since a virus is really only an evil little computer program, it can be eradicated by formatting the infected floppy disc, etc., or by deleting the file containing the virus.

- Make sure you have a clean, i.e. virus free, write-protected boot disc which will allow you to start the computer after a virus attack. A copy of a virus scanner on floppy disc (or ZIP disc or CD) is essential for situations where the hard disc is infected and unfit to use. The original CD provided with Norton AntiVirus can be used as an emergency startup disc.

- Make backup copies of important files when you know they are clean. An infected file can be repaired by overwriting it with a clean version.

- "Booting up" or starting from an infected floppy disc accidentally left in the drive is a common entry route for viruses. In normal use, make sure your computer is set to boot up by reading from the hard disc straightaway, without looking at the floppy disc or CD. Changing the boot sequence is described earlier in this chapter. This precaution is essential when a large number of people have access to computers and are likely to insert their own floppy discs from dubious sources.

- Increasing use of the Internet is providing greater opportunities for the virus writers to create havoc. Always carry out a virus check on all files downloaded from the Internet or received as e-mail attachments, before opening the files to read.

- The compression program WinZip (discussed later) can be set to check downloaded Internet .ZIP files. This is achieved by extracting the compressed files into a temporary folder before scanning them with your own installed virus scanner. Then the temporary folder is deleted and (assuming they are virus free) the downloaded files are extracted and installed onto your hard disc.

- If you install a program like Norton AntiVirus 2002, a memory resident virus scanner will be running in the background, whenever the computer is in use. Such scanners can cause problems during the setup of new software. The memory resident scanner should be temporarily *disabled* (not uninstalled) during the installation of new software.

Compressing Files And Folders

Introduction

The process of compressing files has been around for many years. It was pioneered by software such as PKZIP and in recent years, WinZip from Nico Mak Computing, Inc. The compressed files are generally known as ZIP files. The purpose of compression is to reduce the size of files, thereby increasing the effective capacity of storage media such as hard discs, floppy discs and CDs. While the arrival of hard discs of gigantic size has lessened the pressure for ultra compact storage, there are still advantages to be gained by compressing files:

1   Compressed files can be transmitted much more quickly across the Internet and as e-mail attachments.

2   When transporting files between computers or making security backups on removable media such as floppy disc, ZIP disc or writeable CD, many fewer discs are required.

3   Files which are not used frequently but which may be needed in future can be *archived* effectively by saving them as compressed files.

Compression is achieved by storing the data in the files more efficiently. Some files compress more than others. This is because compression works by picking out common patterns in a file (words like "to" or "the" and spaces, for example) and representing them in a shorter code than normal. So file compression might allow you, for example, to store data on one floppy disc which would otherwise require several.

Previous versions of Microsoft Windows did not contain file compression software. Instead the user had to rely on third party products such as WinZip, mentioned previously. However, Windows XP contains a feature which provides a very simple means of creating ZIP files, involving little more than dragging and dropping files into special **Compressed Folders**. Compressed Folders can also work with ZIP files created by other file compression software such as WinZip. This chapter describes the features of Compressed Folders and also discusses WinZip, which contains many useful features for creating and managing ZIP files, including virus checking using your own anti-virus software (if installed).

Before compressed files can be opened for use they must obviously be expanded to restore them to their original size. This process is known as *unzipping* or *extraction*. Normally, to extract a ZIP file you must have a copy of the extraction program installed on your hard disc. However, it is possible to produce a special type of compressed file which can extract itself. When the new compressed file is created, instead of being saved as a ZIP file, it is saved as an .EXE file. This includes, within the compressed file itself, the program which does the "unzipping".

This self-extracting file may therefore be used on computers without a separate installation of the compression/extraction software. As it is an .EXE file, it can be invoked like any other application, i.e. by clicking on the file name in Explorer. Existing ZIP files can usually be converted to self-extracting .EXE files in software like WinZip, using a menu option.

Although Windows XP provides the Compressed Folders feature, programs like WinZip contain many features which may justify their purchase. A full evaluation copy of WinZip is available over the Internet. (Downloading software is discussed elsewhere in this book). After an initial evaluation period, a registered version can be purchased, on-line if required. Alternatively, you can buy the boxed package from mail order suppliers like Atlantic Coast Software of Colyton, Devon. Several other file compression packages are available from different companies.

Creating a Compressed Folder

The basic method is to create a Compressed Folder in the location of your choice - perhaps within another folder or on the Windows XP Desktop. Any files you wish to compress are then dragged and dropped into the Compressed Folder. To extract (or decompress) the files they are either dragged to a new location and dropped or you can use the Extraction Wizard.

To create a new Compressed Folder within another folder, open up the folder in **My Computer**. Then select **File** and **New** from the menu. One of the options is to create a **Compressed (zipped) Folder** as shown below.

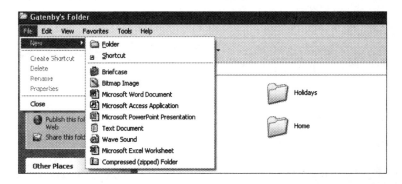

If you select **Compressed (zipped) Folder** an icon for the Compressed Folder appears and you can replace the name **New Compressed (zipped) Folder** with a name of your

New Compressed (zipped) Folder
1 KB

choice, such as **Squashed Files**. A Compressed Folder can be created on the Windows Desktop or in **My Computer** by right clicking over an empty spot then selecting **New** and **Compressed (zipped) Folder**.

Once you have created a Compressed Folder, you can drag files into it in **My Computer** as shown in the example on the next page.

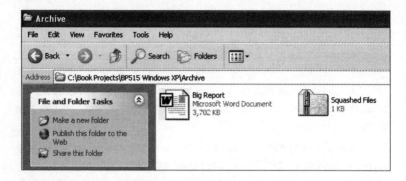

The window above shows a file **Big Report.doc** with a newly created Compressed Folder **Squashed Files** next to it. After dragging the file over the compressed folder, the following situation arises.

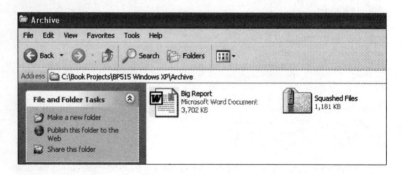

Notice in the above window that the size of the Compressed Folder **Squashed Files** has increased from1KB to 1,181KB. Please also note that after the dragging operation the original copy of the file **Big Report** is still present in its original location.

If you now double click the compressed folder it opens up to show the icon for the compressed version of the file **Big Report**. Right clicking over this icon gives details of the compression process as shown on the next page. You can see that the original file of 3,702KB has been compressed to 1,181KB.

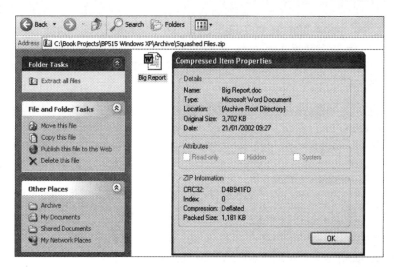

More details of compressed files can be obtained by opening the Compressed Folder in My Computer and then selecting **View** and **Details**.

A quick way to create a Compressed Folder is to right click over a file or folder in My Computer. A menu appears including the options **Send To** and **Compressed (zipped) Folder** as shown below.

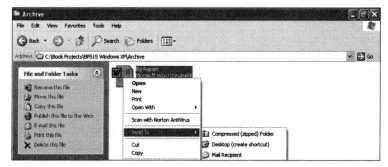

If you choose the **Send To/Compressed (zipped) Folder** options, a new Compressed Folder is created alongside of the original file or folder. The compressed folder has the same name as the original file or folder.

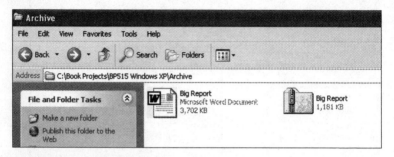

Copying or Moving a Compressed Folder

You can **Copy** (or **Move**) a Compressed Folder to another destination by dragging and dropping using the *right* mouse button. (The right button launches a menu allowing you to choose either **Copy** or **Move**.) This includes copying to a floppy disc. Using the above example, a Word file of 3,702KB was compressed to 1,181KB. This enabled it to be copied comfortably to a floppy disc of only 1440KB capacity.

Adding or Deleting Files in a Compressed Folder

Files can be added to an existing Compressed Folder by dragging and dropping. Files can also be deleted by highlighting the file in the Compressed Folder in My Computer and either pressing the **Delete** key or selecting **File** and **Delete** from the menu bar.

Opening a File in a Compressed Folder

If you double click a file in a Compressed Folder, it will be opened in its associated program. So, for example, if you have compressed a Word document, double clicking the file's icon in the Compressed Folder launches the Word program and opens the relevant document.

Extracting Files from a Compressed Folder

Individual files can be extracted i.e. decompressed, by dragging and dropping into their new location. This could be another folder on a hard disc or a removable medium like a floppy or ZIP disc.

When you extract a file from a Compressed Folder, the compressed version of the file remains behind. If this is a very bulky file, you may wish to delete it from the Compressed Folder.

There is an option to extract all of the files from a Compressed Folder. With the Compressed Folder open in My Computer, select **File** and **Extract All...**. After browsing for or entering the path of the folder (or directory) in which the extracted files are to be placed, the **Extraction Wizard** decompresses the files. The destination for the extracted files could be a removable medium such as a floppy disc, ZIP disc or CD-RW.

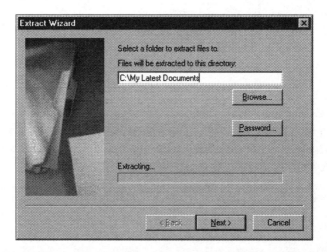

Suppose you transfer a Compressed Folder to another computer, either via a removable medium such as a floppy disc or by sending over the Internet. If the machine is running Windows XP with the Compressed Folders component installed you can extract the files as described in this chapter.

Otherwise the files can be extracted using a file compression program like WinZip, described on the following pages. The Compressed Folder behaves like a normal ZIP (or .zip) file. This can be seen by switching on the file name extensions in Windows XP, which by default are not normally displayed. In **My Computer** or the **Windows Explorer** select **Tools**, **Folder Options...** and then click the **View** tab.

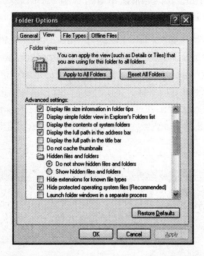

Make sure that **Hide extensions for known file types** is not ticked then click **Apply** and **OK**. If you now select **View** and **Details** in My Computer you can see that the Compressed Folder is listed as a *file* with the **.zip** extension as shown below.

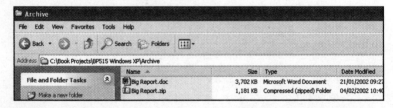

Normally the term *file* refers to a single document saved on a disc. However, a ZIP file (which has the extension **.zip**) acts more like a folder, since it can contain lots of other files in compressed format.

Introducing WinZip

The provision of the Compressed Folders feature in Windows XP may answer many of your file compression needs. However, third party programs like WinZip from Niko Mak Computing, Inc. are worth considering since they have many useful features and are not very expensive. The WinZip program is easy to use yet fast and powerful. You can download a trial version from the Internet from **http://www.winzip.com/** or purchase through the normal mail order suppliers.

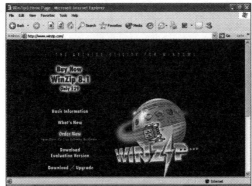

Associating ZIP Files with Applications

Please note that since both WinZip and Windows XP's own Compressed Folders feature can be used to handle ZIP files, you may need to specify which application is to be associated with ZIP files. For a particular ZIP file, right click over the file's icon in My Computer or the Windows Explorer. Whichever application you select here will be used to handle this particular ZIP file when you double click its icon.

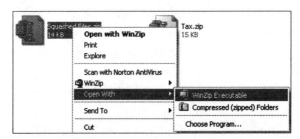

To change the application (WinZip or Compressed Folders) associated with ZIP files in general, enter My Computer or the Windows Explorer and select **Tools** and **Folder Options...**. Select the **File Types** tab as shown below. Scroll down and highlight **ZIP File** and check the line starting **Opens with** followed by the associated application, in this case **Compressed (zipped) Folders**. This can be altered after clicking the change button and selecting a different application, as shown in the right-hand window below.

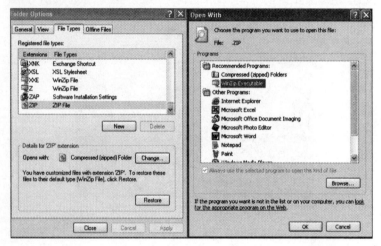

Please note that when WinZip is associated with ZIP files on your computer, ZIP files appear with the WinZip icon shown on the right.

If the Compressed Folders application is associated with ZIP files on your computer, all ZIP files appear with the Compressed Folders icon shown on the right.

If you want to alternate between using WinZip and Compressed Folders, change the file association in My Computer or the Windows Explorer after selecting **Tools** and **Folder Options...** as described above.

Using WinZip

WinZip can be launched from its icon on the Windows XP
Desktop or from the **start** menu, then **All Programs** and
WinZip. Or you can double click its icon (shown right) on the
Windows XP Desktop.

There are two basic modes of operation, namely WinZip Classic and
WinZip Wizard. In WinZip Classic the user is presented with a Windows
style interface with drop-down menus. In WinZip Wizard you are guided
through the various steps after answering questions about what you
want to do, then clicking **Next**.

The WinZip Wizard is particularly useful for searching the hard disc for
ZIP files and adding to the sorted list of **Favorite Zip Folders**.

Please notice that the wizard picks up all of the ZIP files on your hard
disc, including many downloads from the Internet. These are normally
stored by default in the folder **C:\My Download Files**.

Single buttons allow you to easily switch between the WinZip Wizard and the WinZip Classic interfaces. If you have downloaded a ZIP compressed file from the Internet, the WinZip Wizard will take over the extraction of the file and its installation into a directory of your choice.

For creating a new ZIP file or archive, the WinZip Classic interface below is fast and easy to use.

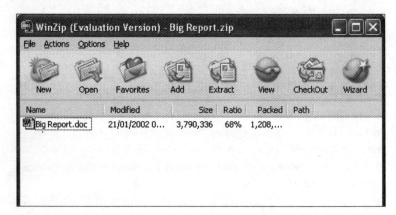

Reading from left to right, the WinZip Classic options shown on the above toolbar are:

Create a **New** ZIP archive. This is a single file, in this case **Big Report.zip** as shown in the title bar. The above ZIP file contains one compressed file, in this case the Word document **Big Report.doc**.

Open a previously created ZIP archive. Individual compressed files may be unzipped and there are various file operations such as copying, moving, deleting and renaming.

Clicking the **Favorites** icon opens up the list of ZIP files on your hard disc. From this you can choose a particular archive to work on.

The **Add** option allows you to browse through your hard disc and add any files to the archive (i.e. ZIP file) which is currently open in WinZip.

Add

Clicking **Extract** expands a compressed file and allows the user to select a destination folder for the extracted file.

Extract

The **View** option allows you to see a selected file running in its associated program. For example, a compressed Word document could be examined running in the Word application. You can also view a file by double clicking on the file name in the ZIP archive. In fact, this extracts the folder into a temporary folder. Later, after viewing in its associated program, the temporary file is deleted from the hard disc.

View

The **CheckOut** feature is used to examine files and programs you have received as ZIP files.

CheckOut

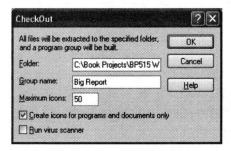

WinZip creates a program group in the main Windows XP menu system accessed from **start** and **All Programs**. Each of the individual files in the archive appears as a menu item.

If the file is a document, clicking its name causes the file to be viewed running in its associated program. The CheckOut feature can also include a virus scan (discussed later).

The last icon on the WinZip Classic menu bar switches control of the program to the WinZip Wizard.

Wizard

Creating a ZIP file in WinZip

The ZIP file is like a folder in that it contains a set of compressed files. These are documents produced in programs like Word, Excel or Paint, etc. Once the archive is created, files may be added or deleted. In this example, a new ZIP file will be created from the following folder, called **Future Plans**, containing documents created in Word, Paint and Excel shown below in the Windows Explorer. (Folders are displayed in the left-hand panel below by selecting **View**, **Explorer Bar** and **Folders**).

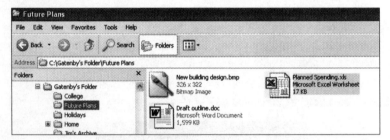

After starting WinZip Classic and selecting the **New** icon from the toolbar, we are asked to select a folder for the new archive to be saved in and give a name to the ZIP file, **Plan 2003** in this case.

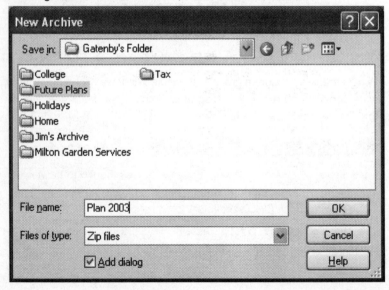

Then we are required to select from our hard disc the files which are to be added to the new archive.

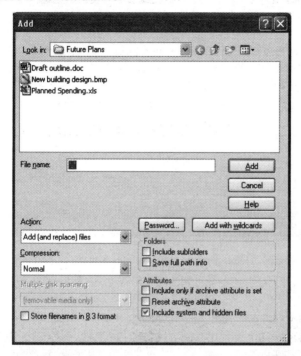

You can highlight an individual file to be added or leave the wildcard *.* to add all files in a folder. Entering *.EXE for example would add all files with the .EXE extension to the new ZIP file.

Note in the above window, WinZip can be used to compress programs according to the state of their *archive bit*. As discussed elsewhere in this book, the archive bit is used to signify if a file needs to be backed up. You could use WinZip to make regular backups and only record files if they had changed since the last backup.

Once we have clicked on **Add**, the WinZip Classic window appears showing the archive containing, in this example, three compressed files. It can be seen that different types of file can be compressed by different amounts.

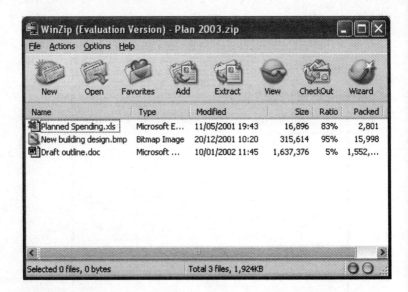

From this archive, you can extract files into a chosen directory, delete them or add new files. Double clicking on a file starts the associated program allowing you to examine a fully working copy of the file.

You can also add files to an existing archive using the Windows Explorer. With the archive open in its window, a file is dragged from the Explorer and dropped over the list of files in the archive. Alternatively, you can select the file in Explorer, then use **File** and **Add to Zip file...**off the Explorer **File/WinZip** menu bar. (Or press the right mouse button over the file name then use **Add to Zip file...**).

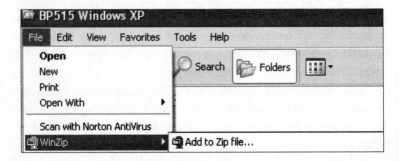

Extracting Files Using WinZip

This is very easy using either WinZip Wizard or Classic. In WinZip Classic open the required ZIP archive and select the files to be extracted. Then you click the **Extract** icon and select the folder into which the extracted files are to be placed.

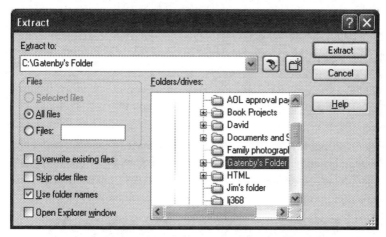

Clicking the **Extract** button above will expand the files and place fully working copies of the files in the selected folder on your hard disc.

Self-Extracting Archives

Suppose you want to take some compressed files and use them on a machine which isn't equipped with a program to extract the files, like WinZip or PKUNZIP or Windows XP with the Compressed Folders feature. The solution is to create a self-extracting archive. This is a compressed file which has an unzip program built into it. The self-extractor has the .EXE extension. This is the format for many of the files downloaded from the Internet. The file is copied into a folder on the hard disc and to unzip or extract the file you simply double click on its file name in the Windows Explorer or My Computer. You can choose the folder into which the unzipped file is to be placed.

To convert a ZIP file into a self-extracting .EXE file, click the drop-down **Actions** menu in WinZip and select **Make.Exe File**.

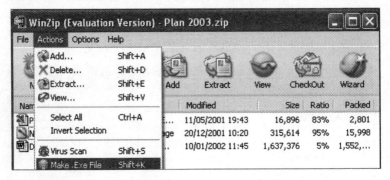

You can specify the directory into which the self-extractor will unzip itself. This may be on another person's computer, if you are using WinZip as a vehicle for transferring files. By default WinZip self-extractors unzip themselves into the user's TEMP= folder.

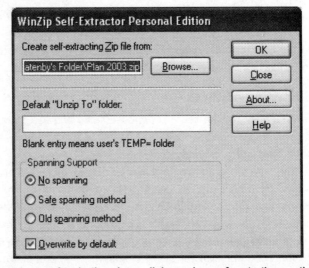

The term **spanning** in the above dialogue box refers to the continuation of a ZIP file over several floppy discs or other removable media.

Using WinZip to Check ZIP Files for Viruses

There are dangers of viruses when downloading ZIP files from the Internet or from floppy discs of uncertain origin. When WinZip is first set up it can detect if your computer has a virus scanner installed.

To carry out a virus scan, click the option on the WinZip **Actions** menu shown below.

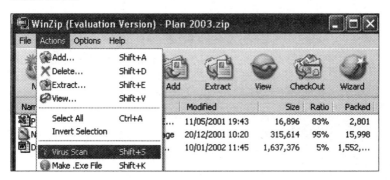

First the ZIP file is extracted, then the files are virus checked *using your own installed virus scanner*. If no virus warnings are given, you know the file is virus-free when you see the message:

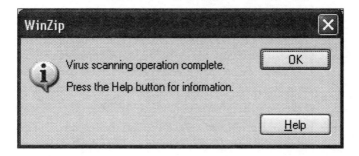

You can also include a virus scan by ticking **Run Virus Scanner** in the **CheckOut** feature of WinZip, as discussed earlier in this chapter.

Summary: Compressing Files and Folders

- Files may be compressed to a fraction of their original size, depending on the type of data. File compression converts common words and shapes into a shorter than normal code.

- File compression allows more files to be stored on a given storage medium such as a removable disc.

- File compression should be used to enable large files to be transmitted quickly around the Internet as e-mail attachments.

- Files which are not used very often may be archived by compressing and storing in another folder. If necessary, the original uncompressed files can be deleted to save space.

- Windows XP introduces Compressed Folders, which are compatible with ZIP files created in programs like WinZip.

- Compressed Folders are easy to create and enable files to be compressed and extracted by simple drag and drop methods.

- In programs like WinZip, a ZIP archive file is created which acts as a folder for compressed files. Files can be compressed by dragging and dropping them onto the ZIP file.

- Files must be uncompressed or extracted before they can be used as normal files in applications.

- Special self-extracting files can be created in programs like WinZip. These have the .EXE file name extension and "unzip" themselves when you double-click on their file name. Self-extracting .EXE files are useful for sending compressed files to people who don't have an "unzip" program on their computer.

- The WinZip Wizard simplifies the extraction of software downloaded from the Internet, as well as installing the software on your hard disc, ready to run.

- WinZip can run a virus scan on downloaded compressed files, after first unzipping them into a temporary folder.

Building Your
Own Network

Introduction

A network allows many people to access the same information and to share expensive software and peripheral devices such as printers and centralised storage and backup facilities. Large networks can be used for internal communication by e-mail and to host an Intranet (an in-house Internet containing pages specific to a particular organisation).

The benefits of networking are not confined to the large organization with hundreds of workstations. Many homes now have two or more computers and lots of small businesses, offices and primary schools have a cluster of several computers (2-10 say) which can benefit from networking, as follows:

- Expensive printers, CDs and scanners, etc., can be shared by all of the computers.

- A single telephone line, modem and Internet connection, can be accessed by every computer.

- Files can quickly be copied between computers - much easier than swapping lots of discs.

- You can communicate with people in different parts of your home, office, school or business premises.

Unlike large networks, which are extremely complex to install and manage, the small "peer-to-peer" network is quite simple - it's basically a case of installing network interface cards in the computers then plugging the cables and connectors together. Windows XP contains all of the networking software you need and also provides the **Network Setup Wizard**. This greatly simplifies the task of setting up a network, enabling the ordinary user to carry out a task which was previously the work of skilled technicians.

Types of Network in Context

There are two basic network configurations - **client/server** and **peer-to-peer**. The peer-to-peer network is perfectly suitable for the home and small office, for whom this book is intended, while larger organizations invariably use the client/server model. For completeness, a brief description of the client server network is given on the next three pages. The remainder of the chapter then covers the setting up of a peer-to-peer network.

The Client/Server Network

The client/server model is used for larger networks - from about ten machines up to several hundred. These may be contained within a single room or scattered throughout a business site or college campus.

At the centre of the network is the server, often referred to as the *file server*. (You can also have *mail servers* and *print servers*.) The server is normally a more powerful computer than the users' workstations (also known as *clients*) distributed around the network. The server and the clients must each be fitted with network interface cards (NICs). These handle the flow of data and provide the connections for the network cabling which links the computers. Networking hardware is discussed in detail later in this chapter.

The server normally has a more powerful processor, bigger memory and larger hard disc(s) than the workstations. This enables the server to carry out its demanding role dealing with the requests from the client machines. These will include running most of the applications software which is used around the network and dealing with printing. It will also act as a central store for everyone's work, such as word processing documents, spreadsheets and other files produced by users of the client machines.

It is normal to buy a special network version of, say, a word processing or accounts program. This software is only saved on the file server machine, but you can run it from any of the client machines around the network. To run multi-user software legally, a licence should be purchased to cover the number of concurrent users of the package.

In education or training a single CD may be licensed and made accessible to all of the machines on the network. This can be achieved using either a shared CD drive or by copying the entire CD onto a special dedicated hard disc, which acts as a CD server.

The server computer may also act as a *print server* to manage shared printing across the network, although nowadays this role is often performed by a dedicated print server - a separate small hardware device which is plugged into the network in a suitable location.

It's normal for the file server machine to be left running continually, including weekends and holidays. This enables users to go online at any time, perhaps from another building on the site. When the server is eventually shut down, this must follow a certain procedure. If the server were to suffer a sudden power failure, the resulting unsupervised shut down may damage the server and its contents. Therefore servers on essential networks are fitted with an Uninterruptable Power Supply (UPS). This keeps the server powered up long enough for a shut down to be carried out according to the correct procedure.

As the server may contain all of the data files for an entire business, security is vitally important. When a server goes down, the whole network is immediately out of action. All data files should be backed up onto magnetic tape every day, with several tapes used in rotation and stored separately.

The client/server model is very efficient for the larger organization, with its centralised resources. However, the client/server model is expensive and a large network (with *hundreds* of computers) requires highly trained IT professionals as network administrators. It really is too complex for enthusiastic amateurs to dabble in. The administrators' work includes the management of users and their login names and passwords, the installation of new software and the scheduling of backups. Also the setting of access rights to files and directories, the removal of obsolete files and protection against virus infection. Apart from troubleshooting any hardware problems there is also the task of staff training. In large organizations, the network staff might also design and maintain a company Web site or create an in-house *intranet*.

Even a client/server network with a relatively small number of machines (10-20 say) will require at least one well-trained member of staff with outside professional support for trouble-shooting and modifications.

The client/server model requires a dedicated network operating system such as Windows NT Server, Windows 2000 Server or Novell Netware and this can cost hundreds or thousands of pounds. Network operating systems provide sophisticated facilities for organising users with login names and passwords and for managing files and scheduled backups.

The cost of the server machine itself must also be considered, since in most cases it will be dedicated to its role as a file server and will not be available for use as a workstation.

The client/server network is a sophisticated and powerful system giving high performance and security. However, it's expensive to manage and maintain and therefore not appropriate for many home and small business users. The next section describes the simple peer-to-peer network which is more suitable for the home or smaller organisation.

The Peer-to-Peer Network

The peer-to-peer network is eminently suitable for connecting a few machines (up to about 10) in the home, in a small office or perhaps a primary school. The peer-to-peer network uses the same basic networking hardware as the client/server model, i.e. cables connecting network interface cards in every machine. However, in the peer-to-peer network there is no dedicated server - all the machines have equal status. Also, there is no need for a special network operating system - everything you need is included within Windows XP.

When the peer-to-peer network has been set up, you can view the computers which are connected, using a feature called **My Network Places**. This can be launched from its entry on the Windows start menu, as shown below.

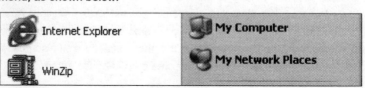

All of the shareable resources on the networked computers appear in a window, as shown below.

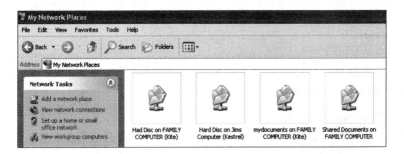

In the above example there are two machines, **Kestrel** and **Kite** in a peer-to-peer network. They are both members of the same workgroup, **Home**. Double clicking on the icon for the hard disc of either machine opens up a window showing its shareable folders. These may be *tiled* as shown below. Folders and files may be copied between machines by dragging and dropping. This is discussed in detail later in this book.

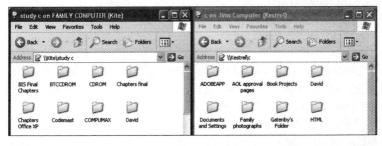

The peer-to-peer network enables operations such as file copying between computers to be carried out much faster than other methods such as using a single cable linking the parallel or serial ports - the Direct Cable Connection. Networking kits designed for the home or small business are becoming available very cheaply. The simplest kit consists of two network cards and all of the necessary cabling and connectors for under £20. Using the networking software included free within Windows XP, this provides a very fast and efficient way of connecting two machines.

While the peer-to-peer lacks the sophisticated management, security and backup facilities of the client/server network, this configuration does have several advantages. For a small number of computers, it's easier to set up and manage and doesn't require specialist computer staff. It is also cheaper since there is no need to dedicate one computer as the server. One disadvantage is that if one computer is used as the print server, the person working at this machine may notice a loss of speed if several people are trying to print at the same time.

Ethernet

Ethernet is a networking standard (used by both client/server and peer-to-peer networks) developed by the Xerox Company in 1976. The Ethernet system includes the network interface cards, the cabling which connects the computers and the *network protocol*, i.e. communication language. Data is transmitted around the network in *packets,* each packet also containing a unique address for both the sending and destination computers. Every packet is delivered to every station on the network. The network cards "listen" for packets containing their address. Only when the station's address matches the delivery address will the data be received by the computer.

Thin Ethernet

The cheapest networking kits (under £20) include two network interface cards and a **Thin Ethernet** cable to connect them. Also known as **Thinnet**, **Coaxial**, **Coax** and **10Base2**, this cable has a single copper centre and **BNC** bayonet connectors at each end. Although computer professionals use crimping tools to make up their own cables, ready-made cables can be purchased from computer suppliers. The cables are connected via T-pieces to the network cards at the back of the computer. In a Thin Ethernet network the computers are arranged along the cable in a line - a configuration known as the **Bus** topology.

This requires each end of the cable to be fitted with a special **terminator**. These should be included in a Thin Ethernet kit but otherwise they are available cheaply from computer stores.

Thin Ethernet represents old technology and is limited to a data transfer rate of 10 Mega bits per second. (8 bits typically being used to represent an alphabetical or numeric character). However, 10Mbps is probably fast enough for most home networks - it seems stunningly fast when copying files. The T-pieces, each having 3 bayonet connections, can be unreliable. In a network of many computers, with the bus technology, any break in the continuity of the cable will cause the whole of the network to fail. This can result in hours of network "down time" until the break is detected. However, in a home environment, especially if cost is a factor, a cheap Thin Ethernet network consisting of two network cards, a Thin Ethernet Cable, two T-pieces and two terminators is all you need to start networking with two machines. The system will work perfectly well over the distances likely to be encountered in the home or small business.

UTP (Unshielded Twisted Pair)

Also known as **10BaseT, UTP** is a later design of cabling used in many modern networks and looks similar to telephone cabling. Plug-in connectors fit into ports in the network interface cards. These ports are known as **RJ-45**s. The core of the cable comprises two copper wires twisted together and this design gives higher performance. Standard UTP cable (**10BaseT**) operates at 10Mbps while a higher specification cable (known as **100BaseT**) has the potential to operate at the **Fast Ethernet** speed of 100Mbps. For operation at 100Mbps, a UTP cable classified as **Category 5** is recommended whereas 10Mbps systems can manage with the inferior **Category 3**.

If you are connecting only two machines you can manage with two network cards containing RJ-45 ports and a special UTP **cross-over** cable obtainable from computer stores.

However, a preferred solution is to connect the machines radially around a central **Hub** containing several RJ-45 ports. The computers are connected by individual cables like spokes around a wheel, an arrangement known as the **Star** topology. A major advantage of this configuration is that you can disconnect an individual computer and cable without disabling the rest of the network.

Complete home networking kits can be purchased from networking giants like 3Com for under £100 and these include the network cards, cabling and a hub containing several RJ-45 ports. You simply plug the UTP cables into the hub in the way that telephone cables plug into a jack socket. (In large organisations computers may be up to 100 metres from the hub and extra hubs or **repeaters** can be inserted to increase the length of an arm of the network).

For the last few years I have been using the 3Com OfficeConnect networking kit designed for the home and small business. It was easy to set up and is fast and reliable. The OfficeConnect hub has several LEDs which give diagnostic information such as the status of the ports and whether or not packets of data are being sent or received. If you wish to expand your network, more hubs can be connected later.

The Network Interface Card

This is a small printed circuit board which connects each PC to the network cabling and handles communication with the other computers on the network. Also known as a *NIC* and a *network adapter*, the term *network card* will generally be used throughout this book. The network card is fitted to a spare expansion slot on your computer's motherboard (the main circuit board to which the principal components are connected).

Fitting the network card is a task which anyone can undertake, without special skills. It's just a case of removing the cover of your machine and plugging the card into one of the free slots on the motherboard. Network cards are available with either Thin Ethernet (BNC) connectors or UTP (RJ-45) ports. "Combo" cards allow both types of cable to be connected. If possible network cards designed for the computer's PCI slots should be obtained as these are easier to configure.

Before starting work you should divest yourself of any static electricity, as this can damage sensitive electronic components like the network card. To prevent this, earth yourself by touching a metal object such as the metal frame of your computer or part of a central heating system.

Alternatively you could wear one of the special earthing wrist straps which are available cheaply from electrical component suppliers. A well-lit room is desirable: it's also useful to have a small torch handy to illuminate the hidden depths of your machine.

With the machine switched off, disconnect all of the cables from the back of the computer. The casing can then be removed, usually after taking out a few small retaining screws. You should see several spare slots of various types on the motherboard as follows:

Long black slots:	ISA architecture
Long brown slots:	EISA architecture
Short white slots:	PCI architecture

The documentation accompanying your network cards should specify the type of slot required by your particular card.

If you have several spare slots all of the correct type, the card can be inserted into any one of them - position is not important. Now remove the blanking plate adjacent to the chosen slot by taking out and keeping safe the single retaining screw. Taking care not to touch the edges of the network card, firmly push it into the slot until the gold edge connectors are evenly engaged. Now secure the card by fitting the retaining screw. Replace the casing and reconnect the cables at the back of the machine.

External Network Cards

If you don't want the inconvenience of opening up your computer, it's now possible to buy external network adapters which plug in to a USB port on the back of your computer. The USB ports are small rectangular slots about 12mm by 5mm. Obviously this is not as neat a solution as the more common internal cards described previously.

PCMCIA Network Cards

Anyone using a notebook (or laptop) computer on the move will probably want to connect to a network on returning to base. Special credit card size Network Interface Cards are available which plug in to a tiny slot on the computer.

These cards are termed PCMCIA (Personal Computer Memory Card International Association), after the computer industry group which agreed on a specification for upgrade cards for portable computers.

PCMCIA cards are very easy to plug in and remove and installation of the necessary software drivers should be automatic. Like many components for notebook computers, however, PCMCIA cards are more expensive than the equivalent ISA or PCI components for full-size desktop machines.

Connecting the Cables

You need to insert network cards in every computer which is going to be networked, before starting to connect the cables.

Before you can configure the network cards you need to install the cabling which links the machines together. If you are using coaxial cable (Thin Ethernet) then you must connect the cable to each machine using T-pieces or Y-pieces and fit terminators to each end of the cable.

If you're using twisted pair (UTP) cabling then each cable should be inserted into the RJ-45 port in a network card, before inserting the other end in an RJ-45 port in the hub. When all of the cables have been connected, the power to the hub should be switched on. A constant green light (LED) against the number for each port on the hub indicates that the card and its associated cabling are correctly installed. There may also be a green light on the network card suggesting that all is well. If there is no green light at the appropriate port on the hub, check that the cables are properly connected and the network card is firmly and evenly located in the slot on the motherboard. Obvious though it seems, it may be necessary to check that the hub is switched on!

The latest Plug and Play technology should ensure that each new network card requires very little setting up before it is ready to start work. If you buy PCI cards then they should be self-configuring. Normally the card is detected automatically when the computer is restarted.

Troubleshooting

All being well the network card is now ready for use, although the network software components in Windows XP still need to be set up on each machine. This is discussed in the next chapter.

If you fit PCI cards, these should be self-configuring and present few problems. However, you may encounter some problems if you fit ISA cards or cards which are not compatible with Plug and Play.

The process of configuring a network card sets various parameters so that the new device integrates smoothly without clashing with other devices already installed in the computer. This includes allocating an *interrupt setting (IRQ)* to the network card. An interrupt setting is the number of a channel which the device uses to communicate with the central processor of the computer. This number must be unique to the device; Two devices (such as a modem and a network card, for example) cannot share the same interrupt number if they are to operate simultaneously. In the past this was frequently a problem during the installation of new hardware, requiring manual adjustment to the interrupt settings. Plug and Play technology is intended to alleviate this problem.

You can check if a device such as a network adapter is working correctly by looking in the **Device Manager**. This is opened by selecting **start**, **Control Panel**, (in **Classic View**) then double clicking the **System** icon.

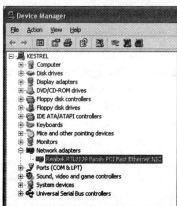

Now click the **+** sign to the left of **Network adapters** to display the name of your particular adapter. Right click over the name of your adapter and select **Properties** from the resulting menu. This shows the **General** tab for the network adapter including a message to say whether the device is working correctly. If not there is a troubleshooter button to help you solve the problem.

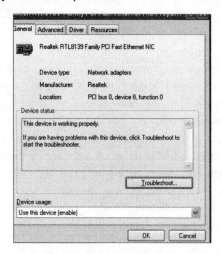

This may include referring you to the Windows Hardware Compatibility List, a Microsoft Web site which checks a component's suitability for Windows XP.

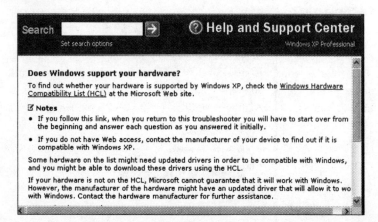

You may need to contact the manufacturer of the network adapter for updated driver software which will enable the device to work with Windows XP.

Clicking the **Resources** tab above gives details of the critical settings of your network adapter including the important interrupt (or IRQ) setting. If the IRQ has been wrongly set to a number already in use by another device a message will appear in the **Conflicting device list** as shown below. (Showing **No conflicts** in this example).

In some situations it is necessary to resolve a conflict by changing the **IRQ**. This is done by switching off the tick against **Use automatic settings** and then clicking the **Change Setting** button. You will then be able to cycle through different settings for the IRQ until **No Conflicts** appears in the **Resources** tab as shown above.

(The above method is used to resolve IRQ clashes on other devices apart from network cards).

Please note that <u>before</u> replacing an old network adapter with a new one, the entry for the old card should be uninstalled from the Device Manager. This is done from a menu which appears when you right click over the entry for the network adapter in the **Device Manager**. The **Device Manager** is opened by selecting **start**, **Control Panel**, (in **Classic View**) then double clicking the **System** icon and clicking the **Device Manager** button.

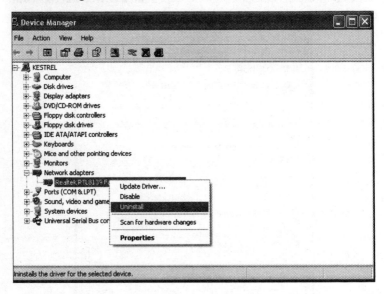

In general, before installing a new device which replaces an old one, the entry for the old device should be uninstalled from the Device Manager. Apart from network adapters, this might, for example, also apply to CD drives. When the new device has been installed, check that a new entry appears in the **Device Manager** and that the new device is working correctly as described on the previous page.

Wireless Networking

This technology has been around for a few years and has many attractions for the home and small business. Windows XP has introduced support for wireless networking in acknowledgement of the increasing popularity of this technology. While not currently offering better performance than wired networks, there are many positive features. Firstly, there are no unsightly network cables trailing around your home or office. You can connect computers hundreds of feet apart in your house or business premises without having to install cables and drill through walls or beams, etc. Apart from being able to share files and printers from remote parts of a building, you can also share a single Internet connection or play multi-user games.

Wired networks in different buildings can be connected by a wireless bridge and you can connect wireless enabled computers to a conventional wired network.

Users of notebook computers have much to gain from wireless networking. The home user can work in the garden while communicating with a computer in the house or further afield on the Internet or on a business network.

Wireless networks normally use an **Access Point**, which acts like a hub in a conventional network (described earlier). Apart from directing network traffic to and from the various client computers on the network, the Access Point also converts data from wired networks into radio frequency data for the wireless clients. Communication is possible over a distance of several hundred feet from the Access Point.

The Access Point is normally connected to the Internet and many large commercial organizations such as coffee bars, airports and railway stations are now installing Access Points throughout their sites. These enable anyone with suitable (i.e. "wireless enabled") notebooks, Personal Digital Assistants (PDAs) and mobile phones to access the Internet or their e-mail and company network.

Each client computer on the wireless network must be fitted with a special wireless network adapter. These are available as PCI cards to be fitted internally to a desktop PC, or externally plugged into a USB port on the back of the computer. If your network consists of only two computers in close proximity, the network adapters are the only extra components you need for wireless networking - you don't need an access point. This configuration is known as an "ad-hoc" network. Wireless networking components are currently more expensive than the parts for an equivalent cable network. However, the cost of cabling and labour must be added to the cost of the conventional wired network.

The leading wireless technology conforms to a standard known **as IEEE 802.11b** or **Wifi** and there is also a competing standard known as HomeRF. **Bluetooth** is the name of a wireless "cable replacement" technology being developed by nine of the world's leading technology companies including IBM, 3Com, Intel and Motorola. Bluetooth allows devices such as desktop computers, notebooks, PDAs, cell phones and digital cameras to communicate with each other and to access e-mail and the Internet. Bluetooth works between devices up to 30 feet apart.

Setting up the Windows XP Networking Software

Before you can start to use the new network there is still some setting up to do in Windows XP. Fortunately Windows XP provides the **Network Setup Wizard**. This makes sure that the correct Windows XP network software components are installed. You also need to ensure that users of the network will be able to share folders and devices such as printers. These topics are covered in the next chapter.

Summary: Building Your Own Network

- Networking enables two or more computers to share expensive resources such as data files, applications software, printers, and CDs. Also to carry out tasks such as file transfer and backups.

- Windows XP contains **Internet Connection Sharing,** software which allows several networked computers to share an Internet connection using one modem and one telephone line.

- The peer-to-peer network connects all machines as equals; they can access each others' applications and data files and share a printer.

- The peer-to-peer network is relatively easy to set up and manage for small networks of 2-10 machines. Windows XP contains all of the software needed to set up a peer-to-peer network, including the newly introduced Home Networking Wizard, which simplifies the process.

- Complete kits are available cheaply and these contain all of the hardware for a peer-to-peer network.

- The client/server configuration is used for larger networks. The server is a powerful machine dedicated to the management of the network and used as a central store for the applications software and data files. A special network operating system is required such as Windows 2000 Server or Novell Netware.

- The client/server network has sophisticated software for security and file management, including backups. These require the skills of a trained network administrator.

- Ethernet is the dominant standard for network technology such as network interface cards and cabling. Thin Ethernet is an older and slower type of cabling which requires computers to be connected in a continuous line, known as the Bus topology.

- UTP is a newer Ethernet specification, with the potential for faster operation, in which computers are connected around a central hub in the Star topology. The hub has diagnostic facilities and allows individual cables and machines to be removed without disabling the rest of the network, unlike the Bus configuration.

- Fitting network cards and connecting the cabling is a simple task which anyone can accomplish.

- If a computer has been previously fitted with a network card, the old card should be physically removed before starting to fit the new network card. The entry for the old card in the **Device Manager** should also be removed, after clicking **start**, **Control Panel** and double-clicking the **System** tab. Select the **Hardware** tab, highlight the name of the network card in the **Device Manager** and click the **Remove** button.

- The installation process involves the copying of driver software for your particular brand of network card. Also the setting of various parameters such as interrupts, to avoid conflicts with previously installed devices.

- PCI network cards are recommended as they are self-configuring and therefore very easy to install.

- The new network card should be detected automatically but if not, Windows XP provides manual methods of detection and installation.

- To complete the installation you may need your Windows XP CD and any discs provided by the manufacturer of the network card.

- The status of the network card can be examined in the **Device Manager**, accessed by **start**, **Control Panel** and **System** icon. This reports on any problems and allows alternative settings to be tried.

- Windows XP includes the **Networking Troubleshooter** for diagnosing and suggesting solutions to a wide range of problems.

- Wireless networking provides neater installations without the mess of cabling or the need to drill through walls. Communication is possible between devices several hundred feet apart.

- Wireless networks can be connected to cabled networks.

- Access Points in public places enable wireless notebook computers and other devices such as mobile phones, etc., to connect to the Internet for e-mail and other services. Bluetooth technology is designed to connect a wide range of wireless devices in close proximity.

Windows XP Networking

Introduction

This chapter describes the setting up of the Windows XP software in order to run a small peer-to-peer network. Before starting work you should have already installed network cards in all of the computers, as described in the previous chapter. Then you should have examined the **Device Manager**, accessed from the **System** icon in the **Control Panel**, by clicking the **Device Manager** button on the **Hardware** tab. The name of your network card should be listed under **Network adapters**. Right click the name of your network adapter and select **Properties** from the resulting menu.

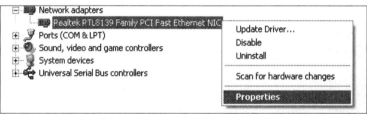

You should see a message to say that the adapter is working properly. If it is not working correctly click the **Troubleshoot...** button to try to solve the problem.

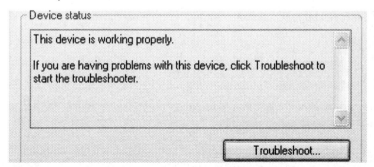

You should also have connected all of the network cards to a hub in the case of a UTP network or to each other in the case of Thin Ethernet cable, as described in the previous chapter. If you are using UTP cabling with a hub, the hub should be switched on and you should see green lights corresponding to each network card.

The next part of the work used to be quite complex in the past and involves checking that each machine has certain networking software components installed. These components have jargon names such as "TCP/IP", "NetBEUI" and "IPX/SPX-compatible protocol". Fortunately, Windows XP includes the **Network Setup Wizard**, which guides you through the setting up of the networking software and shields you from the more technical jargon. The Network Setup Wizard is described shortly.

To check the devices in your home network, select **start**, **Control Panel** (in **Classic View**) then double click **Network Connections**. The resulting window shown below displays both your Internet Connection (**Dial-up Connection**) and the network adapter for your **Local Area Connection**, i.e. your peer-to-peer network.

As shown above left, this window also contains the option **Set up a home or small office network**.

The Network Setup Wizard - An Overview

The next few pages describe the process of setting up the Windows XP software for a small home or business network. One computer, known as the *host*, is connected to the Internet via a modem or other connection. Connected to the host machine via the local area network (either cabled or wireless, as previously described) are one or more computers known as *clients*.

After completing the Network Setup Wizard, all computers on the network should be able to:

- Share files and folders on other computers.

- Share devices such as printers and CDs.

- Connect to the Internet via a single modem or other type of Internet connection.

- Protect each computer from outside "hacking" using the Internet Connection Firewall included in Windows XP.

Sharing a single Internet connection is a major incentive for creating a small network. However, you should check with your Internet Service Provider (ISP) that multiple use of a single connection is allowed.

The basic method is to run the Network Setup Wizard on the Host computer, i.e. the machine which is the physically connected to the Internet. Then, working at a client machine, run the Network Setup Wizard again. Please note that client machines need not be running Windows XP. Apart from Windows XP Professional and Windows XP Home Edition, client machines can also be running Windows 98, Windows 98 Second Edition and Windows Millenium Edition. Although Windows Millenium has its own Home Networking Wizard, you must use the Windows XP Network Setup Wizard to connect a Windows Millenium machine to a Windows XP host machine. At the end of the Windows XP Network Setup Wizard you are given the opportunity to create a copy of the wizard on a floppy disc. This allows you to run the Windows XP Network Setup Wizard on client computers not running Windows XP.

Setting Up the Host Computer

Make sure the Internet connection is working correctly on this machine. Then start the **Network Setup Wizard** after selecting **start**, **Control Panel** (in **Classic View**) then double clicking **Network Connections**.

After clicking **Set up a home or small office network** you are presented with the welcome screen telling you what can be done with a network.

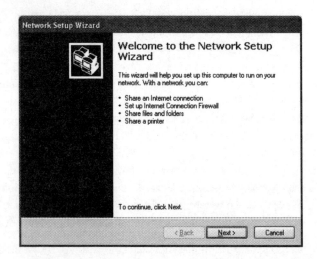

Clicking **Next** displays a window asking you to check that all the preparatory steps have been completed. These include installing the network cards and cables as described in the previous chapter of this book.

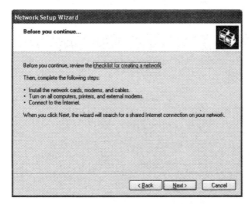

A document giving a full checklist of preparatory steps can displayed and printed at this stage after clicking **checklist for creating a network** as shown in the above window.

After clicking **Next** you are presented with a window which allows you to set up either a host or a client machine.

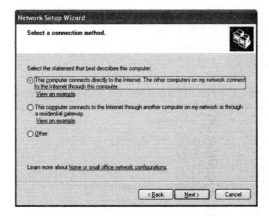

Since we are setting up the Internet host computer, we select the option beginning **This computer connects directly to the Internet.....**

In the previous window, if you are not sure what the various network configurations look like, Windows XP provides explanatory diagrams. These are displayed (as shown below) by clicking **View an example** from the Network Setup Wizard window shown at the bottom of the previous page.

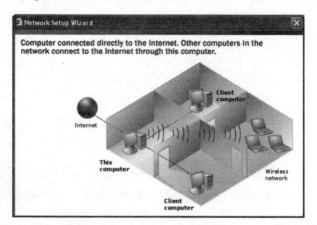

In the above diagram, **This computer** refers to the Internet host computer at which we are currently working. Please also note that one or more computers equipped for wireless networking can be integrated within a wired network.

Moving on through the wizard after clicking **Next**, we can see that the wizard has detected our Internet **Dial-up Connection**, i.e. the **Pace 56 Voice Modem** in this case. Select i.e. highlight the modem.

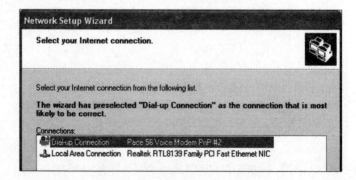

The next window requires you to enter identification for the computer you are currently working at.

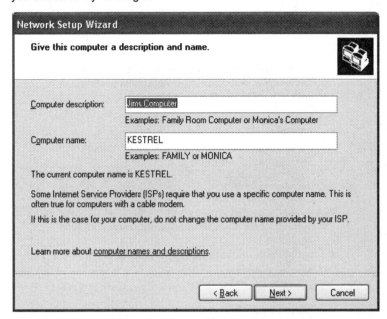

Computer description: Jims Computer
Examples: Family Room Computer or Monica's Computer

Computer name: KESTREL
Examples: FAMILY or MONICA

The current computer name is KESTREL.

Some Internet Service Providers (ISPs) require that you use a specific computer name. This is often true for computers with a cable modem.

If this is the case for your computer, do not change the computer name provided by your ISP.

Learn more about computer names and descriptions.

Computer name must be *different* for every computer on the network. Then you are required to enter a **Workgroup name i.**e. a name for the group of machines on your network that will be sharing the same files and other resources.

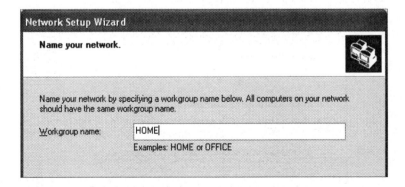

Name your network.

Name your network by specifying a workgroup name below. All computers on your network should have the same workgroup name.

Workgroup name: HOME
Examples: HOME or OFFICE

Before actually applying the settings you have specified, the Network
Setup Wizard presents a summary of your settings:

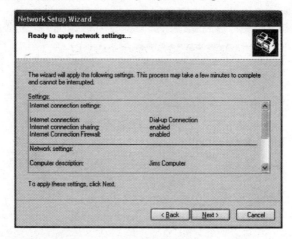

If you are happy with the settings click **Next** and the process of
configuring the computer begins. This may take a few minutes, after
which you are given the chance to create a **Network Setup Disk**.

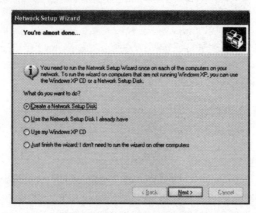

This setup disc is used on client machines running Windows 98,
Windows 98 Second Edition or Windows Me.

The wizard gives you a chance to format the floppy disc before making a copy of the Network Setup Wizard. Then you are given instructions about running the Windows XP Network Setup Wizard from the floppy disc, on those client computers not running Windows XP.

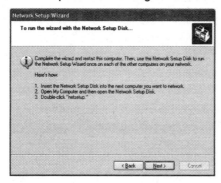

Finally you should be informed that you have successfully set up the host computer for networking.

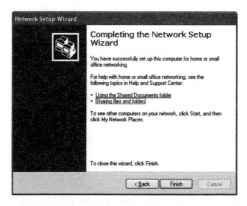

This window also contains links to help pages which explain the sharing of files and folders so that other people on the network can use them. Sharing is discussed separately later in this chapter.

Having set up Windows XP networking on the host machine, the next task is to run the Networking Setup Wizard on the client machine(s). This topic is discussed on the next page.

Setting Up the Client Computers

If you are setting up a client computer which is running Windows XP, the Network Setup Wizard is started from the **Network Connections** window as described on page 166 of this book.

If the client machine is running Windows 98, Windows 98 Second Edition or Windows Millenium, you can use the floppy disc version of the Network Setup Wizard, created during the setup of the host machine, as described on the previous page. Place the floppy disc in the drive of the client machine and select **Start** and **Run**. Enter **A:\NETSETUP.EXE** as shown below by typing or by browsing the floppy disc.

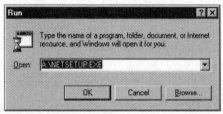

After you select **OK** the Network Setup Wizard will start up and copy some files from the floppy disc. Then the computer is restarted. On restarting the computer, the Network Startup Wizard will start up automatically and the procedure from then on is the same as described earlier for the Windows XP host computer. However, as this is a client machine we need to specify **This computer connects to the Internet through another computer in my network....** as shown below.

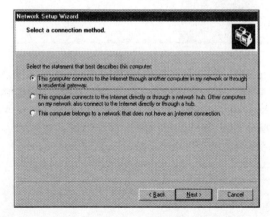

After you have set up your host and client computers you are ready to check that your machines can actually communicate with each other. This is done by selecting **My Network Places** off the start menu.

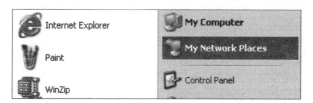

You should see the shareable resources on the machines on your network as shown below.

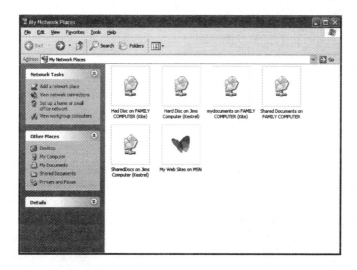

As shown above, this small network has two computers. One is the **FAMILY COMPUTER** named **Kite**. The other is **Jims Computer** named **Kestrel**. These names and descriptions were set up during the Network Setup Wizard described previously. However, they can be altered manually, as described shortly.

During the Network Setup Wizard we had to give each computer a workgroup name and in this example the name **Home** was used. To view the computers in the workgroup, select **View workgroup computers** from the left-hand panel in **My Network Places** as shown below.

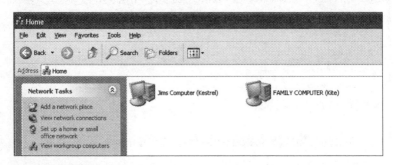

Troubleshooting

If you can't see all of the computers or resources on your network, there are several possible causes:

- The network cards and cables may not have been set up correctly. These can be carefully reinstalled and checked for correct functioning in the **Device Manager**, as described in the previous chapter.

- You might have made an incorrect entry during the running of the Network Setup Wizard on host and client machines. For example, each computer must have a unique **Computer Name**, but they must all share the same **Workgroup**. These can be checked manually and altered if necessary as described shortly. Otherwise you need to run the Network Setup Wizard again on each computer.

- If necessary, start the **Network Troubleshooter** by selecting **start**, **Control Panel** (in **Classic Mode**), double clicking the icon for **Network Connections** and selecting **Network Troubleshooter** from the left-hand panel.

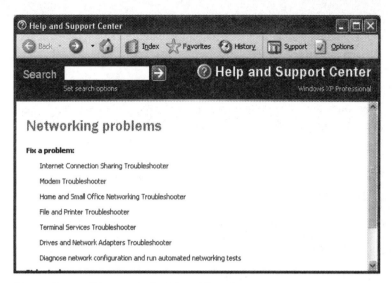

Changing a Computer's Identification

To change the name and workgroup of a computer on your network, select **start** and **Control Panel** (in **Classic Mode**) and then double click the **System** icon. Select the **Computer Name** tab and then click the **Change** button. As shown below on the right, you will now be able to change the **Computer name** and **Workgroup**.

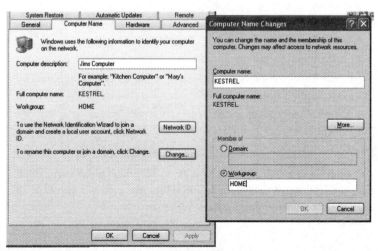

Internet Connection Sharing

Your client machines should now connect to the Internet via the modem or other device in your Host computer. Each client should now be able to run programs like Internet Explorer and Outlook Express. This is made possible by the Internet Connection Sharing feature in Windows XP, which should have been set up during the Network Setup Wizard. You can check the Internet Connection Sharing settings by clicking **start**, **Control Panel** (in **Classic View**) then double clicking **Network Connections**. Highlight your **Dial-up Connection** and select **Change settings of this connection** from the left-hand panel. Now click the **Advanced** tab to reveal the settings shown below.

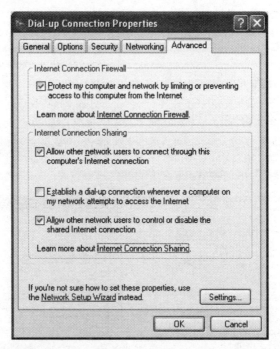

Internet Connection Sharing can be switched on or off using the tick box next to **Allow other network users to connect through this computer's Internet connection**.

The Firewall

The Internet Connection Firewall shown enabled in the **Dial-up Connection Properties** dialogue box on the previous page is a new feature introduced in Windows XP. A firewall is a software device designed to prevent "hackers" attacking your computer from the Internet.

Sharing Resources

In order for all of the computers on a home network to be able to open and modify files on another computer or use a single network printer, for example, these resources must be set up as *shareable*.

Windows XP provides a folder called **Shared Documents** which allows different users to share documents *on the same computer*. Within the Shared Documents folder are the sub-folders Shared Music and Shared Pictures. If a group of people using the same computer (as in a family situation, for example) all want to look at the same documents, these are made accessible to all by dragging and dropping them into the **Shared Documents** folder, using Windows Explorer.

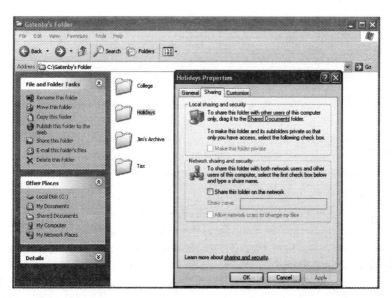

To make a folder or file *shareable on a network*, highlight the resource
in My Computer then click **Share this folder** from the left-hand panel,
as shown on the previous page. Now select with a tick **Share this
folder on the network**.

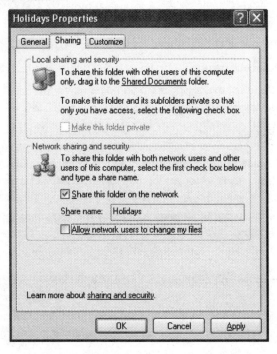

You must also provide a **Share name** by which the resource will be
known on the network. Please note that there are security risks here if
you are working with important files. Even if you are happy for other
people to view the files you might at least want to switch off the option
Allow network users to change my files shown above.

If you feel there is no risk to your data, for example if only one or two
people have access to the network and you trust them with your files,
then you may wish to make entire hard discs or CD drives shareable.
Right click the hard disc or CD drive in **My Computer** and select
Sharing and Security... as shown on the next page.

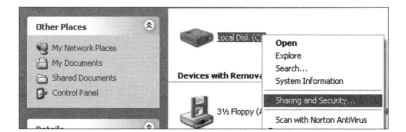

You are warned of the risk of sharing the entire drive (the "root" or root directory) as shown below.

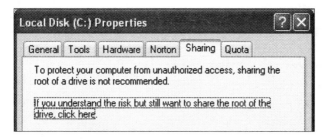

On accepting the risk and clicking the message above, you are presented with the **Properties** dialogue box as shown on the previous page. Here you can switch on sharing and give the shared resource a network name. (A disc is still referred to as a folder in this situation).

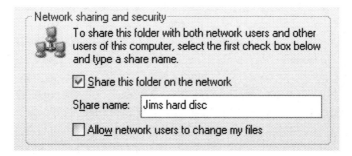

After resources have been successfully made shareable, a hand appears under their icon in My Computer or the Windows Explorer.

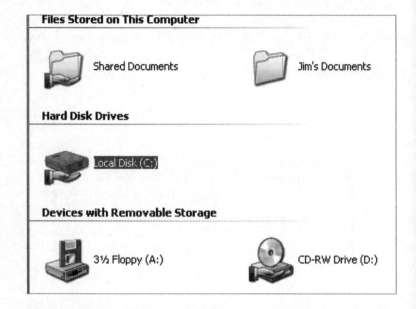

Sharing a Printer on a Network

This is one of the major benefits of a network. It's not cost effective to have a separate printer attached to every computer on the network, apart from the amount of desk space taken up by multiple printers. Printing is an activity which we carry out spasmodically, on completion of a document. So there's no great inconvenience when several computers are connected to one printer on a small network. Normally the printer is attached to the host computer, i.e. the one directly connected to the Internet, although this is not essential.

Before the printer can be shared by other computers on the network it has to be designated as *shareable* in a similar way to the sharing of files, folders and disc drives discussed earlier.

To make a printer shareable select **start**, **Printers and Faxes**, highlight
the required printer and select **Share this printer** shown in the left-hand
panel below. (The fact that the names of several printers are shown in
the window below does not mean several physical printers are
connected to the computer - the icons representing printer driver
software which has been installed on this computer for various
purposes. For example, the Acrobat Distiller is not a physical printer but
a "driver" i.e. software used to make Acrobat PDF files - a file format
which can be read on any sort of computer, including Apple Macintosh.
This book was printed from Acrobat PDF files).

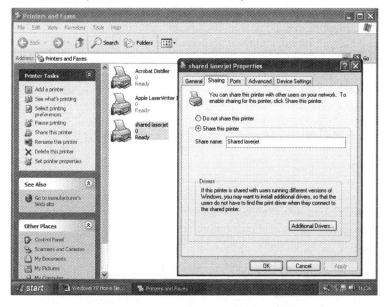

After clicking **Share this printer** the **Sharing** tab/dialogue box appears
as shown on the right above. Here you switch on **Share this printer**
and give the printer a **Share name**. Please note that this operation only
makes the printer *available* for sharing. We must still set up the shared
printer on each client computer (i.e. computers not attached to the
printer) as discussed on the next page.

Please note that, referring to the previous **Sharing** tab, if a client machine is not running Windows XP you may wish to install additional drivers after clicking the **Additional Drivers…** button.

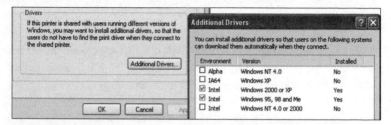

Connecting to a Printer on Another Computer

This section describes the method for setting up network printing from a machine which does not have a printer attached.

Select **start**, **Printers and Faxes** and **Add a printer** from the left-hand panel. This starts the **Add Printer Wizard** shown below.

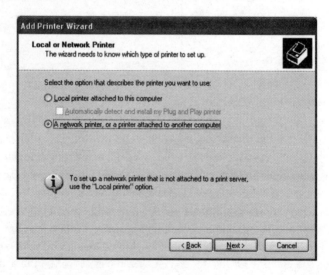

Select **A network printer, or a printer attached to another computer**, as shown above.

On clicking **Next** you are required to **Browse** to find the network printer on another computer (the host usually).

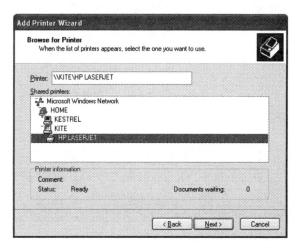

In the example above, it was necessary to double click on the computer name **KITE** to reveal the name of the attached printer, **HP LASERJET**. Select this printer and the network path to the printer should appear in the **Printer:** bar as shown above (**\\KITE\HP LASERJET**). Click **Next** to complete the **Add Printer Wizard**.

After repeating this procedure on all of the computers not directly connected to a computer, you should be able to print from any machine on the network. Without shared printing you would have to use the network to copy files to the hard disc of the computer with the printer attached. Without a network you would need to copy files on to a floppy disc then take the disc to the computer with the printer attached.

I have used printer sharing on a small home network for a number of years. It is fast, reliable and very convenient.

Using the Network

The way you use the home or small business network will vary depending on what your computers are used for. My home network is used mainly for researching and writing books like this one. When you have two or more computers connected on a network, it's extremely easy to make a backup copy onto another machine's hard disc. This only takes a few seconds and I do this regularly - every few minutes. Using this method (together with weekly backups to CD), I have managed to survive the last few years without ever losing a single file of work.

Saving Your Work on Another Computer on the Network

While working on a document in Word or Excel for example, select **File** and **Save As…**.

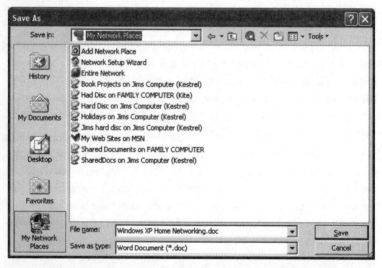

Now select **My Network Places** in the **Save in:** dialogue box. You can now select a location to save your work on another computer on your network. The folder or disc drive will need to have been designated as shareable as discussed earlier in this chapter. After clicking the **Save button** and saving, select **File** and **Save as…** again to revert to saving on the computer you are sitting at.

Copying Files to Another Computer on the Network

You may need to copy a lot of files and folders from one computer to another. Open **My Computer** and highlight the files or folders to be copied.

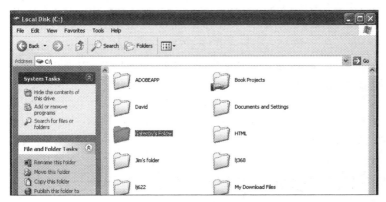

Now click **Copy this folder** from the left-hand panel and the following window appears, allowing you to select the location into which the selected files and folders are to be copied. To copy files onto a hard disc on another computer select **My Network Places** as shown below.

You can use the **Make New Folder** button shown above to save in a new location on the other computer. (Please note that there is also an option to **Move this folder** in My Computer, shown in the top screenshot. Moving should be used with care, since it causes the file or folder to be removed from its original location.)

Another way to copy files between two computers on the network is to open up the hard disc drives for each computer in **My Network Places**, accessible off the **start** menu. Then right click over an empty spot on the Task Bar at the bottom of the Windows XP screen and select **Tile Windows Vertically** from the resulting menu. On my network, two adjacent windows showing the two computers **Kite** and **Kestrel** appear, displaying the folders on each hard disc.

Folders can be moved or copied between the two computers by dragging and dropping. If you drag a folder with the right mouse button held down, when you release the button you can choose whether the file is to be copied or moved as shown above. Select whichever action is appropriate.

Opening a Document from Another Computer

Suppose you want to use your computer to work on a document saved on the hard disc of another computer on the network. In an application like Microsoft Word, simply select **File** and **Open...** then select **My Network Places** and locate the file on the other computer. After selecting **Open** the file will open in your computer from where it can be edited, saved (on any computer) and printed.

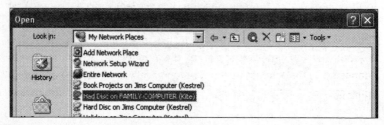

Connecting Client Computers to the Internet

This section describes how the client machines (which don't have their own direct connection to the Internet), can share a connection on another computer. The machine with the modem (or other device) is known as the host machine and manages requests for information from the client machines. When the requested information is received back from the Internet it is relayed from the host computer back to the clients.

Before you can connect a client machine to the Internet via your host computer, you must be sure that the following work (described in the previous chapters) has been successfully completed.

- The host machine (but not the client machines) has Windows XP Internet Connection Sharing enabled.

- The host machine and all of the client machines are connected on a functioning Local Area Network, consisting of network cards and cabling (except in the case of a wireless network).

- The Network Setup Wizard has been run on the host computer and all client machines. In the wizard, the appropriate type of Internet connection (either direct via a modem or via the Local Area Network) should have been selected.

- Each machine should have been identified with a *unique* Computer Name and a *common* Workgroup Name.

- The host machine has a connection to the Internet via a modem or other device and this is working correctly.

You should now be able to connect to the Internet by launching your Web browser such as Internet Explorer, using any machine on the network. Obviously the host machine must be up and running but it does not need to be currently on-line to the Internet. When connecting to the Internet from a client machine, the modem (or other device) on the host machine will dial the telephone number of the Internet Service Provider and make the connection to the Internet. When finishing an Internet session, shutting down a client machine which has been connected to the Internet may not automatically shut down the Internet connection on the host machine. This may need to be done manually.

IP Addresses

The next pages describe how computers are identified on the home network and on the Internet. The IP address is part of TCP/IP, an acronym for Transmission Control Protocol/ Internet Protocol. It can be thought of as a language or set of rules which allows computers of different types to communicate on a network, such as the Internet.

When we log on to an Internet computer using a *Domain Name* like **http://www.gatenby.co.uk/**, this is actually converted to an IP address having the form:

207.168.98.7   (Fictitious example)

We are spared the need to remember IP addresses by the use of the more user-friendly Domain Name for Web sites and e-mail addresses. The host machine on a home/small business network acts as a Gateway for the client machines around the local network. It has a fixed IP address itself but allocates dynamic addresses to the other machines on the network each time they log on.

You can check the IP Address in Windows XP by double clicking **Network Connections** in the **Control Panel**. Highlight the network adapter and select **Change settings of this connection** from the left-hand panel. The **Local Area Connections Properties** window appears.

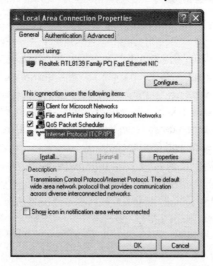

If you highlight **Internet Protocol (TCP/IP)** as shown in the previous window and select **Properties**, the following window appears showing the IP address of the computer.

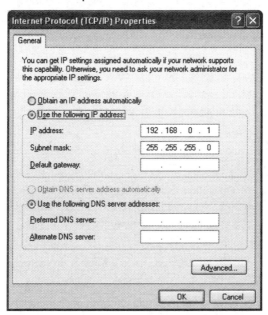

Please note that the above dialogue box represents a host computer with a fixed IP address, i.e. **Use the following IP address** is selected. Client machines would normally have their IP address allocated by the host machine, each time they log on to the network, so **Obtain an IP address automatically** would be selected as shown above. Fortunately these settings are taken care of automatically by the Network Setup Wizard but advanced users often experiment with different IP addresses in order to solve network problems.

Even if you never need to change the IP addresses on your computers it may be useful to have a basic understanding of the way network computers are identified. At least you will not be blinded with science if anyone is talking about TCP/IP, etc.

Summary: Windows XP Networking

- Windows XP contains all of the software needed to set up and manage a home/small business network. This includes a new feature, The Network Setup Wizard. You must have already fitted network cards, etc., to all of the computers.

- All of the computers on the network are shown in **My Network Places**, accessed from the **start** menu. Each computer and its shareable resources can be viewed in its own window from every other workstation on the network.

- Resources must be designated as *shareable* in My Computer to be accessible to multiple users on the network.

- Copying files and folders can be carried out quickly and simply by "dragging and dropping" between the windows of different computers, displayed simultaneously on the screen. Or you can use **Copy this folder** in **My Network Places**.

- Files from other computers can be opened and saved using normal **File** and **Open...** and **File** and **Save As....** Select **My Network Places** in the **Look in:** or **Save in:** bar.

- In order to share a single network printer, each workstation must be individually set up using the **Add Printer Wizard** invoked from **start**, **Settings**, **Printers and Faxes** and **Add a Printer**.

- The Network Setup Wizard also sets up Windows XP **Internet Connection Sharing**. This allows several computers to use a single modem, telephone line and Internet connection. Each client machine connects to the Internet via the local network and the host machine, i.e. the computer with the modem directly attached. All machines connected to the Internet are identified by an individual IP Address. This is a number allocated automatically by the host or gateway computer, when you log on to the Internet. It is also possible to enter IP Addresses manually.

Installing a New Modem

Introduction

The traditional analogue modem (which plugs into a standard telephone line) is still the most popular method of connecting to the Internet, certainly for the home user. There are faster "broadband" alternatives such as cable modems and ADSL (discussed later), but currently these are relatively expensive and are not yet available to users in all areas of Britain. ISDN technology provides some improvement in performance over the 56K modem and is described later in this chapter.

Whereas the conventional 56K modem has a nominal data transmission rate of 56 kilobits per second, cable modems can exceed a rate of one megabit per second. Power hungry applications such as the "streaming" (i.e. broadcasting) and downloading of video files require this extra speed. In the long-term therefore, the analogue modem is likely to be superseded by the more powerful broadband systems. However, the take-up of broadband technology in Britain has so far been extremely slow and the humble modem is expected to be in widespread use for several years to come.

This chapter discusses some of the features of the latest analogue modems and then describes fitting a modem to a computer. Windows XP makes this task very easy and the work really can be carried out by anyone - you don't need any special skills or equipment.

With the latest modems, communications can involve much more than the transfer of data files between computers. Apart from transmitting graphics, fax and sound, telephone messaging systems and video conferencing are now possible between two computers equipped with modems. Even if your computer already has a modem, it may be one of the earlier, slower models and you may wish to consider replacing it as described later in this chapter.

Choosing a Modem

One of the most important factors when choosing a modem is the speed of operation. Clearly, the faster the modem, the less time required to search the Internet or to download large audio, video or graphics files to your computer's hard disc. For a given communications activity, with a faster modem your connection charges should be lower.

The speed of a modem is normally measured in kilobits per second (Kbps). (A bit is a binary digit (0 or 1) and 8 bits are used to represent a character such as a letter of the alphabet). Currently the "56K" modem has replaced its slower predecessors which evolved over recent years with successive speeds of 14.4, 28.8 and 33.6K. (1"K" being approximately 1000 bits).

56K is a *nominal* data transfer rate - the actual rate may be less due to the telephone lines being busy and technical limitations. With the new 56K modems, *uploading* (or sending) from your computer is currently limited to 33.6K or 45K while *downloading* (or receiving) may achieve speeds closer to 56K.

Slow Internet connecting and browsing speeds are a cause of much frustration amongst users. So modem manufacturers have devoted a great deal of effort to improving modem performance.

V.90 Modems

In recent years there were two competing standards for the 56K modem; the x2 technology from US Robotics and the K56flex standard from the Rockwell group. Initially these standards were incompatible, but an agreement between the manufacturers resulted in the V.90 standard, which resolved the conflict between x2 and K56flex.

56K modems could be upgraded to the V.90 standard by downloading a *Flash Upgrade* from the Internet site of the modem manufacturer. This process consists of replacing the modem's operating software, which is stored in a special bank of memory inside the modem. This "flash" memory can be overwritten with new program instructions whenever an upgrade is available.

V.92 Modems

Although at the time of writing V.90 modems are still available and can be obtained for as little as £10, the later V.92 standard brings about several improvements to the analogue modem. While the V.90 standard only permitted *uploading* (i.e. from your computer to the Internet) at 33.6 Kbps, the V.92 standard introduces a feature called **PCM Upstream**, which performs at a more useful 45 Kbps.

Secondly the V.92 standard introduces a feature called **QuickConnect** which reduces the time for establishing a connection between modems, since a V.92 modem "learns" from previous calls to the same modem, so that some initial "handshaking" activities don't need to be repeated.

The **Modem on Hold** feature allows Internet sessions to be briefly interrupted while you answer a telephone call on the same line. Then you can return to browsing the Internet without losing the connection. This avoids the need to set up an extra telephone line for accessing the Internet or to worry about missing important telephone calls while you are surfing the Web. Finally there is a new compression standard called **V.44** which results in faster Internet browsing.

Some V.90 modems, such as those from U.S.Robotics, are upgradable to the V.92 standard by a software download from the Internet. To achieve the improved speed and new features available with the V.92 standard, your ISP must be using compatible equipment - otherwise your modem will be limited to the lowest common speed.

When choosing a modem you should consider the functions you will need; the latest voice modems have answerphone and messaging facilities, in addition to fax and Internet access. You can also use a small microphone to enable complete hands-free voice communication, removing the need for a telephone handset. One small modem can therefore streamline your desktop by replacing several bulky devices.

Modems (together with a suitable camera) can be used for *video conferencing* although it must be said that the quality of the video is very basic. Modems can distinguish between different types of incoming communication - data, fax and voice. Some modems can function independently when the computer is switched off - allowing faxes and voice mail to be dealt with at all times.

The External Modem

An external modem sits on your desktop and requires a plug for its own power supply lead. A disadvantage of the external modem is that it adds to the clutter on your desk. Fitting an external modem is easy, you simply plug it into the outside of the computer without the need to remove the computer's metal casing. Most new computers are provided with two *serial* or *communication* ports - designated as COM1 and COM2. The ports have connectors at the back of the computer into which you plug the cables for peripheral devices like the mouse and an external modem. COM1 is often used to attach the mouse through a 9 pin connector. COM2 is located adjacent to COM1 and is frequently used with a 25 pin connector for an external modem.

External modems are also available which plug into one of the small rectangular USB slots on the back of the computer. These are generally more expensive than external modems connected to the serial port.

The external modem has an array of indicator lights which report on the current activities - whether the modem is switched on, if it is sending or receiving data, fax or voice mail, etc. The external modem is portable - it can easily be unplugged and transferred to another computer.

The Internal Modem

This takes the form of an expansion card which fits inside of the computer. Modern internal modems now use a PCI slot inside of the computer as described on page 153, although there are still some ISA modems in use. To fit an internal modem you therefore need a spare PCI slot inside of the machine and to be happy to remove the casing of your computer and press the card into place. Since the internal modem has no case, no separate power supply unit and fewer cables, etc., it is usually cheaper than the equivalent external device.

The internal modem is tidier than the external model and shielded from accidental damage. Although it's not portable like the external model, it doesn't add to the bird's nest of cables at the back of the machine. You don't need to provide a power point, as you do for the external device. Internal modems contain their own COM port and this is automatically configured as COM3 or COM4.

The Modem Installation Process

The task of fitting a modem is not difficult nowadays and really can be carried out by anyone. Even the internal modem only requires you to undo a few screws to release the casing and then plug the modem card into a vacant PCI expansion slot. Fitting the external modem is even easier - you only have to connect a few cables between the modem and the back of the computer.

The Control Panel

The Control Panel is used a great deal in the setting up and removal of hardware and will be referred to frequently throughout the next few pages. There are several Control Panel *applets* i.e. small programs represented by icons, which are used in this work and they are shown in the screenshot below. Start up the Control Panel from **start**, **Control Panel** and then click **Switch to Classic View** from the left-hand panel.

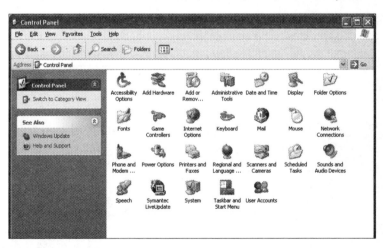

As shown above, the main icons used in the modem work which follows are **Phone and Modem...**, **System**, **Add Hardware** and **Network Connections**. Double click the appropriate icon to launch any of these features. If you prefer to use the **Control Panel** in **Category View** then from the left-hand panel above select **Switch to Category View**.

Removing an Existing Modem

If you are replacing an old modem with a new one, you will need to remove the software for the old one before physically removing the old modem. If you're fitting a new *external* modem, you can easily overlook the fact that an old *internal* modem is still hiding inside of the computer. The old modem would cause problems with the new installation if not properly uninstalled.

The software for the old modem is removed using the **Device Manager**, launched by clicking **start**, **Control Panel** and double clicking the **System** icon, as shown on page 195. Now select the **Hardware** tab and click the **Device Manager** button. Click the **+** next to **Modems** and right click the name of your modem to reveal the menu shown below.

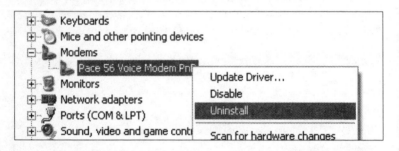

Click **Uninstall** as shown above and the software for the old modem will be removed. Another way to remove the modem software is to launch the **Control Panel** in **Classic Mode**, as described on page 195, then double click the **Phone and Modem Options** icon.

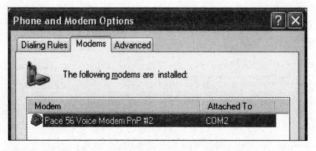

Highlight the name of the modem and click the **Remove** button.

Now shut down the computer and switch off the power. Physically remove the old modem by undoing the cables in the case of an external modem. In the case of an internal modem, undo the small retaining screws and remove the case. Rid yourself of static electricity by touching the frame of your computer, touching water pipes or wearing an anti-static earthing strap. Now undo the single retaining screw and gently pull the old modem out of the PCI or ISA slot.

Fitting a New Modem

Make sure the computer is shut down and any previous modems have been properly uninstalled as just described. The modem manufacturers usually provide adequate instructions and it is usually impossible to fit any of the cables the wrong way around. In the case of an internal modem, divest yourself of static electricity and remove the case of your computer. If necessary remove one of the blanking plates and carefully push the modem card into a vacant PCI slot. Make sure the card is fully engaged. Fit a retaining screw to the modem card and replace the case of the computer.

Detecting the Modem

Windows XP has been designed for *Plug and Play* installation of new hardware devices like modems. So when you restart your computer, Windows XP should detect the new modem, as shown by a small notice which appears at the bottom right of the screen.

An external modem needs to be already switched on before Windows XP can detect it on start up.

Installing the Modem Software

With true Plug and Play devices, Windows XP should find and install the necessary software from its own resources. This is not the case with modems. If you open the **Control Panel** as described on page 195 and double click the **Add Hardware** icon, you will start the **Add Hardware Wizard** as shown on the next page.

On starting the **Add Hardware Wizard** you are advised to switch to your hardware manufacturer's installation CD, as shown below.

Click **Cancel** and insert your modem manufacturer's installation CD. Although setup procedures vary for different products, the general principles are similar. The CD should start up automatically ("autoboot") on being placed in the drive. Then you may need to select the modem installation program from other options on the CD.

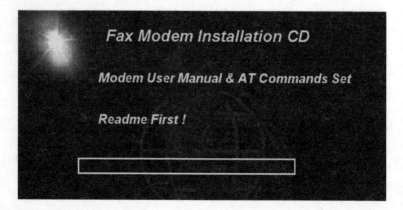

From now on it's simply a case of following the manufacturer's instructions on the screen. These mainly involve clicking **Next**, entering your name and company, if applicable, agreeing to the manufacturer's conditions and accepting or specifying a folder for the modem software. You normally need to restart your computer to complete the installation of the software.

Examining the New Modem

There are several checks that you can do to ensure that the new modem is correctly installed in your computer. Open the **Control Panel** in **Classic Mode** as described on page 195. Now double click the icon **Phone and Modem...** to reveal the **Phone and Modem Options** window shown below. Click the **Modems** tab.

As shown above, the **Generic SoftK56** modem has been installed and attached to the **COM3** port. Right click the **Properties** button to obtain more information about the new modem, as shown in the **Properties** window on page 201.

Another place to check for the presence of the new modem is in the **Device Manager**. From the **Control Panel**, double click the **System** icon then select **Hardware** and **Device Manager**. You should see an entry for **Modems** which can be opened up by clicking the adjacent **+** sign.

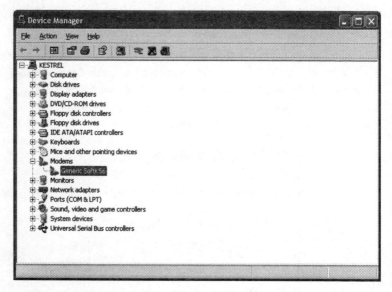

In this case the new modem, **Generic SoftK56** is listed. If your new modem does not appear as shown above or in the **Phone and Modem Options** window shown previously you need to go through the installation procedure again. In the case of an internal modem, make sure the modem has been fully and evenly inserted into the PCI slot. (Care should be taken not to use excessive force). In some cases inserting the modem card into a different PCI slot may solve the problem. If an external modem is not listed in the **Device Manager** or **Phone and Modem Options** then check all cable connections and make sure there is power getting to the modem, indicated by a red light on the modem.

Restart the computer and check for the presence of the modem in the **Device Manager** or **Phone and Modem Options**.

A further check of a new modem is to look in the **Properties** window. This is opened by right clicking over the modem's name in the **Device Manager** shown on the previous page. Then select **Properties** from the drop-down menu which appears.

The above window is also accessible from the **Properties** button in the **Phone and Modems Options** window shown on page 199. Notice that the **Properties** above contains the statement **This device is working properly** and there is also a button to the modem troubleshooter.

A further test is to select the **Diagnostics** tab and click the **Query Modem** button. If the word **Success** appears under **Response** you know all is well.

Interrupt Settings

An interrupt is a request from a peripheral device (like a modem) to the processor, asking the processor to give it some attention. Each device - modem, sound card, printer, mouse, etc., has a line along which it can send an interrupt request (IRQ). Each IRQ line is assigned a number in the range 0-15 (usually assigned automatically by Windows XP during installation or but can be assigned manually by advanced users).

The IRQ number is used by the processor to decide which request to deal with next. Consequently no two devices which are likely to be used simultaneously can have the same IRQ. This applies, for example, to devices such as a mouse and a modem.

Normally with modern computers there is no need to get involved with such complexities - everything should be taken care of automatically. However, should you suspect that two devices are in conflict because they are both trying to share the same interrupt setting, you can check these from the **Properties** window on the previous page. Click the **Resources** tab and you can see the critical settings for the new modem.

You can see above that the **Generic SoftK56** modem has been allocated interrupt **IRQ 12** and there are **No conflicts** in the **Conflicting device list**.

If you want to see a complete list of the interrupt settings for the whole of your computer, from the **Device Manager** select **View** and **Resources by Connection**. Now click the **+** sign next to **Interrupt request (IRQ)** and the full list of IRQs for the computer is shown. The new modem is at the bottom listed as (**PCI) 12 Generic SoftK56**.

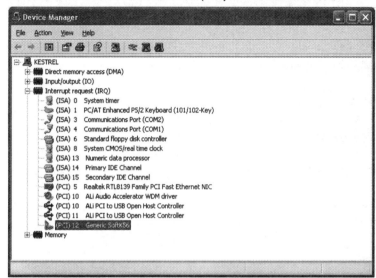

All being well your new modem will have appeared in the **Device Manager** list and the **Phone and Modem Options** window and there will be no conflicts.

We now need to check that the modem can actually dial a telephone number so that it can dial up and connect to your Internet Service Provider. If you have not yet created a *dial-up connection* to an ISP, this is covered in the next chapter. You can still test the dialling ability of your modem using a program called **Phone Dialer**, discussed shortly.

If you already had a dial-up connection to an Internet Service Provider using a previous modem you will probably find that it still exists and has been modified automatically to include the new modem.

You can check your existing dial-up connections in the **Control Panel** in **Classic Mode** (as described on page 195). Double click **Network Connections** and an icon for the dial-up connection should appear along with any local network (**LAN**) connections.

In the above example, double clicking the MSN icon dials up the number of the MSN computer and makes the connection, indicated by

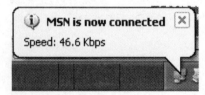

two overlapping monitors on the taskbar at the bottom right of the Windows XP screen.

If you have not yet created a dial-up connection you can still test your modem using the **Phone Dialer** program mentioned earlier. Select **start** and **Run...** then enter **dialer** (using the American spelling) as shown below.

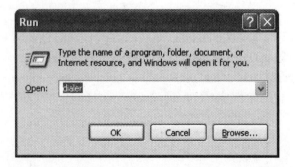

When you click **OK** the **Phone Dialer** window opens as shown below, allowing you to click the **Dial** icon (top left) and enter a telephone number. I find it convenient to enter the number of a mobile phone on the desk in front of me.

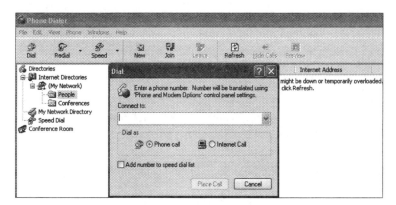

Click **Phone Call** and **Place Call** and if your modem is working correctly you should hear your modem dialling the telephone number.

Modem Troubleshooting

If your modem fails to dial, try starting the **Modem Troubleshooter** after double clicking the **Network Connections** icon in the **Control Panel**, as shown on page 195. Then click **Network Troubleshooter** followed by **Modem Troubleshooter**. The troubleshooter attempts to identify and solve the problem based on your answers to various questions, as shown below.

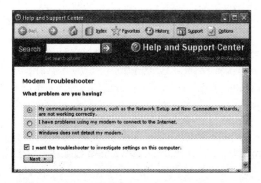

Possible Causes of Modem Problems

- If the modem won't dial, check all of the cables. Connect a telephone handset to the modem (if possible) and check that you can dial a number manually.

- Sometimes the cable between the modem and the telephone line is faulty. Make sure it is the right cable for your modem.

- In the case of an external modem connected to either COM2 or the USB port, the connecting cable inside of the computer may never have been plugged into the motherboard (i.e. the main circuit board of the computer).

- The COM2 port or the USB port may not be "enabled" i.e. set up in the computer's CMOS, which stores all of the basic settings. Entering the CMOS setup feature is described on page 120 of this book. On my computer the port settings are in the **Feature Setup**. The COM2 and USB ports are listed as **OnBoard Serial Port 2** and **OnBoard USB Function** respectively. Make sure the port you are using for the modem is not set as **Disabled**. Cycle through the various alternative settings using the **Page Up** and **Page Down** keys. Consult the handbook for your computer's motherboard for further information on CMOS settings (also known as BIOS settings).

- In the case of an internal modem, the modem card may not be properly seated in the PCI slot on the computer's motherboard. Carefully refit the modem card to eliminate this problem.

- The modem itself may be faulty or incompatible with Windows XP. Check in **Find compatible hardware and software for Windows XP** in **start/ Help and Support**. To access this you must connect to the Internet using another computer.

- The modem might be conflicting with another device on your computer - check in the **Device Manager** as described earlier.

Once your modem is set up you can install any communication software packages which came with the new modem, such as fax and voice messaging. With Windows XP you already have Internet Explorer to browse the Internet; alternatively you may choose to install another browser such as Netscape. If you are new to the Internet, you may also need to install software to connect you to an Internet Service Provider (ISP) such as the Microsoft Network (MSN) or America Online (AOL). This software may be included in the package with your new modem; alternatively it's often given away on the CDs on the front of magazines. These usually include a number of hours free Internet access. These topics are covered in the next chapter "Connecting to the Internet".

The ISDN Alternative

The purpose of a modem is to convert binary digits coming out of the computer into analogue or sound signals for transmission along the telephone lines and vice versa when receiving data into the computer. This translation activity requires error checking and correction operations. The whole process is therefore slower than one in which the communication lines are able to handle data in digital form. Even with the fastest modems, demanding activities such as downloading large data files from the Internet may be very time consuming.

ISDN (Integrated Services Digital Network) is one solution in the quest for higher speeds when transferring data, voice and video data across networks. ISDN is already in widespread use in businesses where large data and graphic files must be conveyed quickly and accurately. Until recently, the high cost of the equipment and running costs put ISDN out of reach for the typical home or small business user. The higher cost of ISDN relative to the modem is offset by the fact that communications are executed faster, with a consequent reduction in connection charges. There are two standards relating to the speed of an ISDN network:

- Basic rate ISDN operating at up to 64Kbps.

- Primary rate ISDN operating at up to 1.920Mbps.

The basic rate ISDN service is aimed at the home and small business user while larger organisations use the primary rate. It's possible to combine two 64Kbps basic rate lines to give communication speeds of 128Kbps, much greater than possible with the fastest modem.

Basic rate ISDN works by utilising your existing telephone cable link to the local telephone exchange. There may be problems, for example, if the cable is an older type made of aluminium rather than copper. (The higher speed primary rate ISDN used by large businesses employs optical fibres). Some telephone exchanges are not yet supporting ISDN. Therefore it's worth checking with your telephone company before spending any money to upgrade your system to ISDN. Also check that your Internet Service Provider is geared up to provide an ISDN service.

To connect to an ISDN network your computer must be fitted with either an ISDN Card (instead of an internal modem) or a Terminal Adapter (instead of an external modem). These can now be purchased for roughly similar prices to a modem.

A common problem in many homes is the single telephone line. If someone is reading their e-mail, surfing the net or sending a fax from the computer, the line can't be used for ordinary telephone calls. The BT Home Highway ISDN 2e scheme not only solves this problem but also provides the digital communication required by ISDN.

The original analogue phone line is converted into two lines which can each use digital or analogue data. The lines can be used in various combinations: one can be used as a conventional phone or fax line while the other acts as a 64K ISDN line. Alternatively you can integrate both digital lines to give an ISDN speed of 128K. Or both lines can be used for analogue phone or fax activities. A small amount of work by a BT engineer is required to install Home Highway.

The Future

The traditional modem is not powerful enough for "streaming" (broadcasting) video across the Internet and the latest V.92 standard may be near the limit of the modem's potential. The future is therefore with "high bandwidth" or *broadband* systems such as the ADSL and cable modem systems currently being introduced. These systems have so far not ousted the traditional modem for many users because they are more expensive and the broadband connections are only available in certain areas.

ADSL

This is an acronym for Asymmetric Digital Subscriber Line, a system which converts ordinary copper phone lines into high speed digital lines. These are capable of handling demanding multimedia applications such as video on demand, multiplayer games and telecommuting with a corporate network. ADSL systems are always on-line to the Internet.

ADSL can download at speeds up to 8Mbps and upload at up to 1Mbps. This compares with a *maximum* of 56Kbps for the conventional modem and 128Kbps for ISDN. A major advantage of ADSL is that it utilizes millions of existing telephone lines, already in place.

Cable Modems

A cable modem is a special device which connects to cable television lines, rather than telephone lines. While potentially being a hundred times faster at connecting to the Internet, the main drawback compared with ADSL and the conventional modem is the limited number of TV cables currently installed. The higher speed for downloading video, graphics, photographs, etc., is coupled with better performance when surfing the Internet. Downloading (to your computer) using a cable modem can be carried out at 3-10Mbps. Uploading speeds (from your computer) are in the range 200Kbps-2Mbps. (Most Internet data traffic is in the downloading direction.) A file which takes 8 minutes to download with an ordinary modem takes 2 minutes on ISDN and 8 seconds using a cable modem. Cable modems are always on-line.

Summary: Installing a New Modem

- An analogue modem is a device for converting between the digital data used by computers and the analogue sound data traditionally conveyed by telephone cables.

- The latest modems conform to a standard known as V.92 and handle data at speeds up to a maximum of 56Kbps. Flash upgradeable modems can be modified by downloading software from the Internet.

- Some modems can support voice-mail, messaging and video conferencing, as well as e-mail, fax and accessing the Internet.

- The external modem is easy to install and is portable while the internal version is neater and cheaper.

- Windows XP offers Plug and Play, a system which greatly simplifies the installation of devices like modems. Both the modem and the computer must be of recent design and Plug and Play compatible.

- Modems are connected to the computer through devices known as communication ports or serial ports. External modems frequently use COM2 while the internal version often uses COM3 or COM4.

- Problems occur when the modem conflicts with another device set to use the same Interrupt Request Setting (IRQ).

- ISDN is a faster but more expensive alternative to the modem. Working entirely with digital data, it is popular with businesses. Most domestic telephone lines can be modified to use ISDN. The cost of converting to ISDN has fallen considerably in recent years.

- The increasing use of the Internet to download and stream (broadcast) massive audio and video files demands more powerful devices than the 56K modem. Fast broadband systems currently being introduced, such as ADSL and cable modems, should eventually become more widely accessible and affordable to the general user.

Connecting to the Internet

Introduction

Before starting the work described in this chapter you need to have installed a modem or other Internet connecting device and ensured that it's working correctly. Then the computer can be connected to the Internet as described on the pages which follow.

When Windows XP is installed on your computer, two of the main Internet tools are included. These are the Web browser Internet Explorer, used for surfing the World Wide Web and the e-mail program Outlook Express. Their icons should appear on the **start** menu as shown on the right.

The computer with its Internet connection might be used on its own to browse the Internet, send e-mail, play games or shop on-line, for example. Additionally this single Internet connection can be shared with other computers connected on a home or small business network as described earlier in this book. Internet Connection sharing is a feature of Windows XP and is discussed in Chapter 9, Windows XP Networking.

Before starting the process to connect to the Internet, you must first choose an Internet Service Provider (ISP). This is a company with fast and powerful computers (known as *servers*) directly connected to the Internet. The ordinary user connects to the Internet via the ISP servers, typically using a modem and the telephone lines. Much faster systems such as ADSL and cable modems are available (in some areas), as discussed in the previous chapter. These "broadband" systems are also much more expensive than the traditional modem, which remains the first choice for most home users.

Choosing an Internet Service Provider

Typically you pay the ISPs for their services by a monthly subscription, although in the last few years there has been a spate of "free" connection services. To avoid receiving enormous telephone bills, connection to the Internet must be available at the *local* telephone rate.

When you start to set up a connection to the Internet using Microsoft's New Connection Wizard, you are presented with a choice of companies. These fall into two categories, **Online Services** and **Internet Service Providers**. The **Online Services** are provided by companies such as America Online and The Microsoft Network (MSN). Apart from enabling you to browse the World Wide Web and send e-mails, these services contain their own news, entertainment and information pages which are only accessible to subscribing members.

Some **Internet Service Providers (ISPs)** offer a specialist connection service to the Web, without the information pages produced by the Online Services. Many of the Internet Service Providers offer a free evaluation period and you will need to give your credit card details at the outset. If you don't wish to continue at the end of the evaluation period you need to cancel your membership to avoid charges.

CDs containing Internet connection software are often provided free on the front of magazines and in shops and supermarkets. Or you may receive Internet free trial CDs in the post, if your name and address have found their way onto the Internet Service Provider's mailing list.

Some criteria for choosing an Internet Service Provider might include:

- Speed and reliability when connecting to the Internet.
- Telephone access numbers available at *local* telephone rates.
- The monthly or yearly subscription charges.
- The number of e-mail addresses per account.
- The quality and cost of the telephone support service.
- Support for the latest technology (such as 56K V92 modems)
- In the case of Online Services providing content, the quality and quantity of the pages of information - news, sport, travel, weather, etc., and their value for research and learning.
- The amount of Web space available for subscribers to create their own Web sites and any charges for this facility.
- Parental controls over children's access to inappropriate Web sites.

It's very easy to be confused by the large number of competing deals offered by the Internet Service Providers. A good source of help is the computing press, which regularly publishes helpful comparisons of the various ISPs and their charges. If possible talk to people who have experience of using various Internet Service Providers.

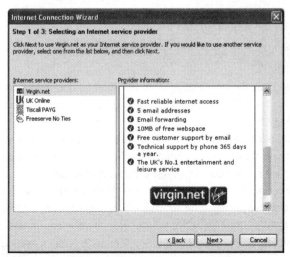

Making the Connection - An Overview

This section assumes your computer has Windows XP installed and the modem is up and running. It is also assumed that your computer has an Internet browser such as Microsoft Internet Explorer or Netscape Navigator. There are several ways to make a new connection with an Internet Service Provider. All of them require you to provide the same basic information, i.e. your name and address, telephone number and credit card details.

During the creation of the new connection you will set up a *User Name*, i.e. the name you use to log on to the Internet. You will also create or be assigned a unique *password*.

There are several ways to launch the process of connecting to an Internet Service Provider. You can use a free CD from the Internet Service Provider or you can use the **New Connection Wizard** in Windows XP. Additionally, if you know the telephone number of your chosen ISP and have obtained a **User Name** and **Password** the connection can be set up manually.

Creating an Internet Connection Using a Free CD

Place the CD in the drive and wait for it to start up automatically ("autobooting").

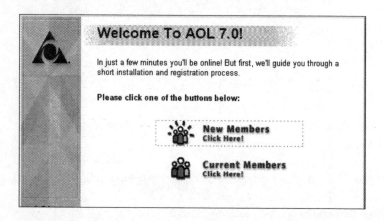

You will be asked to enter a temporary **User Name** (perhaps called something else like a **User ID** or a **REG NUMBER**). You may also be asked to enter a temporary password. This information is normally printed on the cardboard case of the free CD. With this information you will be able to connect to the ISP and enter all of your personal information and credit card details. You should also be able to set up your own personal **User Name** and **Password** and one or more e-mail accounts. At the same time make a note of the telephone number for cancelling this Internet account, particularly if it is a time-limited free trial which you may not wish to continue at the end of the trial period.

Using the New Connection Wizard

If you haven't obtained a free CD there are two ways to proceed. Obtain a User Name, Password and a telephone number for your chosen Internet Service Provider and set up a dial-up connection manually. Or use the **New Connection Wizard** in Windows XP to obtain a list of ISPs in your area. Then choose an ISP and complete the new connection by entering all of your details on-line. Either way the process can be started by launching the **New Connection Wizard** from **start**, **Connect To**, **Show all connections** and **Create a new connection**.

The welcome screen for the **New Connection Wizard** appears, informing you that the wizard helps you to:

- Connect to the Internet.
- Connect to a private network, such as your workplace network.
- Set up a home or small office network.

On clicking **Next**, the wizard presents a choice of the types of connection shown on the next page.

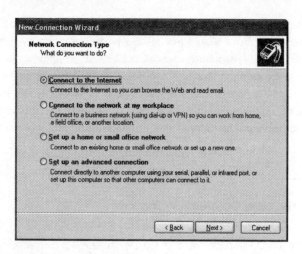

After selecting **Connect to the Internet** and clicking **Next** you are asked to choose a method by which to set up your Internet account.

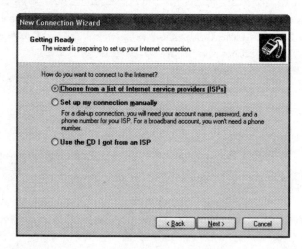

The first option above, **Choose from a list of Internet service providers (ISPs),** is described in detail over the page and involves connecting to the Microsoft Internet Referral Service for a choice of available Internet Service Providers.

The second option, **Set up my connection manually**, in the **Getting Ready** dialogue box on the previous page, requires you to already know your User Name, Password and the connection telephone number of your Internet Service Provider. This method is discussed shortly.

The third Internet connection setup option is to use a CD from an Internet Service Provider as discussed on page 214. In this case you would quit the wizard and insert the autobooting CD.

Setting Up an Internet Connection from a List of ISPs

After choosing the first option in the dialogue box at the bottom of the previous page you must select between:

- **Get online with MSN**.
- **Select from a list of other ISPs**.

Choosing the first option will take you to the sign-up procedure for the Microsoft Network. Taking the second option will create a temporary dial -up connection to the Microsoft Internet Referral Service, shown below.

If you double click the dial-up connection labelled **Refer me to more Internet Service Providers** your computer will be connected on-line to the Microsoft Internet Referral Service.

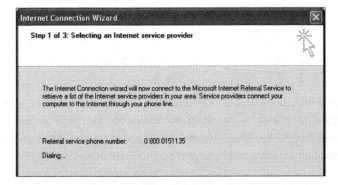

11 Connecting to the Internet

A list of Internet Service Providers available in your area is given, with details of their services.

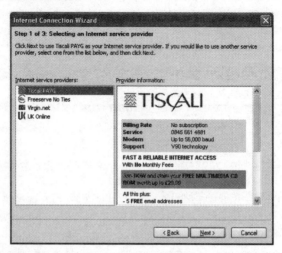

If you select one of the ISPs in the left-hand panel above, then click **Next** you are presented with a form requesting your name and address, etc. The same form appears no matter which ISP you have selected.

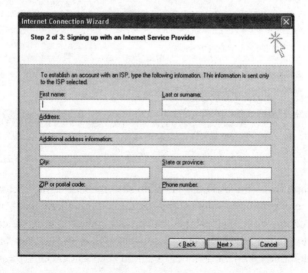

When you have completed the form you will be connected to the ISP server computer where your User Name and Password are set up and you will be required to give details of your credit card. You may also be able to choose, from a list, the phone number which your computer will use to connect to the Internet Service Provider.

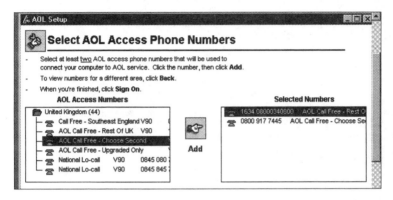

You are advised to check with your telephone company that all Internet connections will be charged at the *local rate*. If you're a BT subscriber, you might wish to add your ISP's phone number to your list of BT Friends and Family frequently-used numbers attracting discounts. On completion of the process you should have a dial-up connection to your chosen Internet Service Provider.

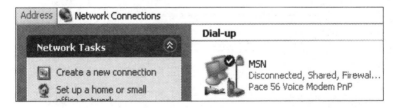

The hand under the dial-up connection shown above right indicates that other computers on my home network can share this Internet connection. The tick indicates that this is the default dial-up connection, used to connect to the Internet whenever you launch a Web browser like Internet Explorer or an e-mail program such as Outlook Express.

Setting Up a Dial-Up Networking Connection Manually

From the **New Connection Wizard**, as shown on page 216, select **Set up my connection manually**. After clicking **Next** you are required to select your type of connection, which for most people will be **Connect using a dial-up modem**.

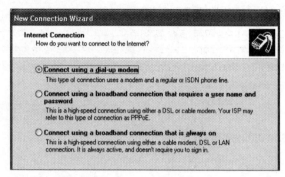

Then you must enter the name you wish to give to the dial-up connection, as it will appear in your **Network Connections** window. After entering the telephone number to connect to your Internet Service Provider, you enter your **User Name** and **Password** which must have been obtained previously.

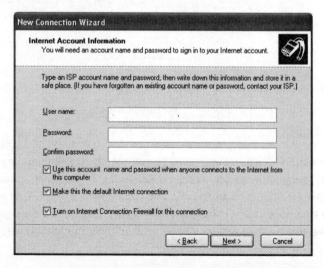

The previous dialogue box also provides the opportunity to make this the default Internet connection and to switch on the **Internet Connection Firewall**. The firewall feature in Windows XP is intended to prevent "hackers" from using the Internet to access and possibly damage the contents of your hard disc.

Using Your New Internet Connection

At the end of the process, the dial-up connection to the Internet which you have created can be seen after double clicking **Network Connections** in the **Control Panel** as described on page 195 of this book.

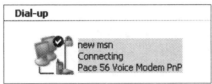

When you launch Internet Explorer to connect to the Internet, the default dial-up connection will appear, as shown below.

In the above example **new msn** is the name of the **Dial-up Connection,** of which there could be several, selectable from the drop-down menu. The setup process should identify the best telephone number for your modem to dial. This must connect to the Internet at *local* telephone rates. The setup process may also include the creation of an e-mail account with your own e-mail address, discussed later.

Changing your Dial-up Settings

At some point you may wish to change details such as the number your modem dials to connect to your Internet Service Provider. To examine or modify your dial-up settings, click **start** and **Connect To**.

To examine the settings on a particular dial-up connection, click the name such as **MSN** shown above. This launches the **Connect** dialogue box in which you can change your password and the phone number to be dialled to your Internet Service Provider. If you change the phone number here and click, you will be asked if you want to make the new phone number permanent - otherwise the connection will revert to the old number next time you try to make a connection.

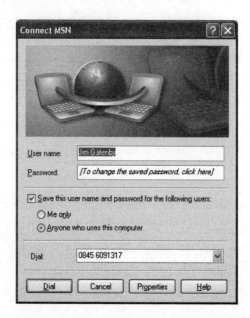

If you select **Show all connections** as shown in the screenshot at the top of the previous page, the following window appears, showing all of your dial-up connections.

Right-clicking over a particular connection launches the drop-down menu shown on the right. Amongst the options are **Connect**, which can also be achieved by double clicking the icon for the dial-up connection. If you are connected to the Internet, the **Status** button will not be greyed

out and this gives details such as the speed of the connection. **Create Shortcut** allows you to place an icon for the dial-up connection on the Windows XP Desktop.

If you click **Properties**, as shown in the menu above, the resulting dialogue boxes allow you to permanently change the phone number used to access your Internet Service Provider, shown below left in the **General** tab.

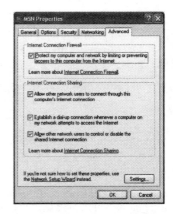

The **Advanced** tab on the right above allows the **Internet Connection Firewall** to be switched on or off. Various options for **Internet Connection Sharing** on a local area network (LAN) are also available.

Summary: Connecting to the Internet

- Getting on-line to the Internet requires a computer linked to the phone lines by a modem or other connecting device, together with an account with an Internet Service Provider (ISP).

- The choice of ISP involves considerations such as monthly subscription, charges for telephone support, information content provided and space for members own Web sites.

- The setup process is often carried out using CDs supplied free by the ISPs, on magazines, in stores and by mailshot. Many of these offer a free trial for a limited number of hours on-line.

- The setup process includes the selection of a telephone number to connect to the ISP at the cost of a local call. Also the entry of personal information such as name, address and credit card details.

- A personal user name must be chosen and this may be used both to log on to the Internet and as part of your e-mail address. A suitable password must also be chosen.

- The New Connection Wizard in Windows XP offers choices of ISP and guides you through the setup process. This can also be done manually if you already have a User Name and Password and an ISP connection phone number.

- The creation of an Internet connection results in an entry in the **Network Connections** window. This is known as a *dial-up connection* and includes your user name and password and the telephone number of an Internet Service Provider. You can have multiple dial-up connections on your computer.

- A dial-up connection to a Local Area Network can also be made. This would, for example, allow someone to access the network at their place of work, for the uploading or downloading of files or to access information.

- Adjustments to connection settings can be made at a later time after selecting **start**, **Connect to** and **Show all connections**.

- Once the connection has been set up you can browse the Internet using Internet Explorer or Netscape, etc., or send e-mails as discussed in Chapter 13 of this book.

Using the Internet

Introduction

The World Wide Web is a collection of billions of pages of information covering every conceivable subject. A *web site* is a collection of related pages, belonging to an individual person or an organization. The Web pages are stored on many thousands of computers, known as Web *servers*, scattered all round the world. In order to retrieve information from the Web, we must first log on to the Internet and then connect to the Web server containing the relevant pages. A program called a *Web browser* is used to move about the Internet and to view and retrieve information. The most commonly used browsers are Microsoft Internet Explorer (part of Microsoft Windows) and Netscape Navigator, part of the Netscape Communicator suite of programs.

In some circumstances, it may be enough to simply view a Web page on our computer screen. Alternatively, all or part of the Web page can be downloaded from the Internet and stored on the hard disc of our own computer. Then the information can be viewed at any time in the future while working *offline*, i.e. without having to connect to the Internet.

If you find a Web page which you think may be useful in future, a link to the page can be saved as a *bookmark* or *favorite*. To return to the page at a later date, log on to the Internet and click the bookmark or favorite. This should connect your computer to the required Web page. Although bookmarks and favorites normally only save *links* to Web pages, rather than the content of the pages themselves, the **Favorites** feature in Internet Explorer has an option to allow a page to be viewed off-line.

Apart from viewing Web pages to research a particular subject, some Web pages enable programs, i.e. software, to be downloaded and stored on your computer. This is now a common way of distributing software, often on a "try before you buy" basis, where you can use the program free for the first 30 days. Further use of the software requires a payment, the whole transaction being completed over the Internet. These topics are discussed in greater detail in the remainder of this chapter.

Connecting to a Web Site

One of the biggest problems with the Web is finding the information. The information is almost certainly out there somewhere, but how do we locate it? A key part of any Web page is the **URL** or **Uniform Resource Locator**. This is a unique address which identifies the page on the World Wide Web. For example,

http://www.mycompany.com

http:

Hypertext Transfer Protocol. This is the *protocol* or set of rules used by Web servers. Another popular protocol is **ftp** or File Transfer Protocol.

www

This means the Web site is part of the World Wide Web.

mycompany

This is the location of the Web server computer hosting the Web site. Usually a company or organization.

com

This denotes a Web site owned by a company. Other common *domains* are **edu** for education and **org** for non-profit making organizations.

An individual Web page within a Web site can be identified by adding its file name to the URL. For example:

http://www.mycompany.com/index.htm

index.htm or **index.html** is the name normally given to the Home Page on a Web site.

If you already know the URL of the required Web site, the task is relatively simple. For example, a company or organization will often give the address of its Web site on its stationery or advertising. Simply type the URL into the **Address** bar of Internet Explorer and click the **Go** button on the right or press the **Enter** key.

Both Internet Explorer and Netscape Navigator maintain lists of recently visited sites, which can be viewed by clicking the down arrow to the right of the **Address** or **Location** bar. Clicking an entry in the list returns you to the Web site. You can enter a URL while working off-line. On pressing **Enter** the browser will connect to the Internet and find the Web site.

If you don't know the address of the required Web page or site, then there are countless search tools available. These produce a list of Web sites which match the key words you typed in.

Using the Address Bar for Searching

Search tools, normally accessed via the **Search** button in your browser, are discussed in detail shortly. However, you can also carry out a search using the **Address** bar in Internet Explorer. Just type your key words into the **Address** bar and click **Go**. The results of the search can be presented in various ways, depending on the settings in **Tools**, **Internet Options** and **Advanced**, as shown below.

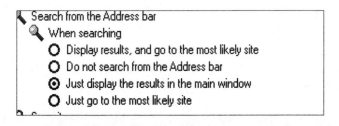

Searching the Internet

There are billions of pages of information stored on the World Wide Web. Whatever topic you want to look into, no matter how obscure, someone is likely to have uploaded Web pages about it. However, without a little knowledge about searching methods there can be frustration and wasted effort.

To search for information on the Web, we enter *key words or phrases* into a search program like Google shown below. Google is a very powerful and popular "search engine" and can be accessed from **http://www.google.co.uk**.

Suppose you have the pleasure of seeing a woodpecker in your garden and want to find out more about it. Entering the key word **woodpecker** returns an unwieldy list of 152,000 Web pages, each containing the word woodpecker.

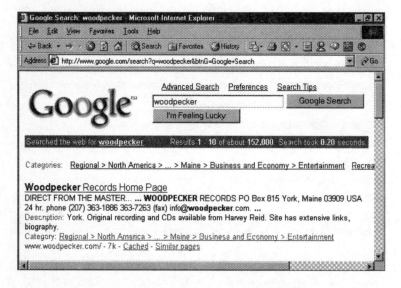

The problem is that by typing simply "woodpecker", we have found **152,000** pages where the word occurs, *in some context or other*, often in the name of some product being advertised.

Very many of the pages found have no relevance to our quest for information about the species of bird. We therefore need to find ways of *refining the search* to eliminate the irrelevant answers.

One strategy is to enter more key words, narrowing down the search. If, for example, **greater spotted woodpecker** is entered, the search tool finds a greatly reduced, but still massive, 13,200 results. This is because the search program finds all pages containing the key words *anywhere on the page* and *in any order*. So, for example, a page containing the irrelevant (in this context) **Heart-spotted Woodpecker**, **Greater Racquet-tailed and Bronzed Drongos** is also listed.

Untitled
... We came across one loose flock containing Heart-**spotted Woodpecker**, **Greater** Racquet and Bronzed Drongos, Asian Fairy Bluebird and Yellow-browed Bulbul. ...
www.ee.princeton.edu/~vivek/trips/Kerala99.html - 16k - Cached - Similar pages

In the bird example, we can narrow down the search much further by entering **"greater spotted woodpecker"**. The addition of the inverted commas ensures that only pages containing the key words *in the given order*, in the exact phrase, will be found. This modified search found only 247 (but highly relevant) results.

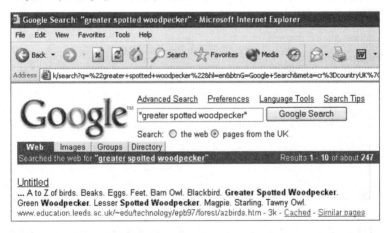

So you can see that minor "tweaks" to the search criteria, i.e. key words, can greatly affect the quality and quantity of the results of a search.

Search Tools

Many of us start searching the Internet by clicking the **Search** button on a Web browser such as Internet Explorer or Netscape Navigator. On Internet Explorer, there is also a **Search** bar on the main Internet Explorer screen and **Search/Search the Internet...** off the **start** menu.

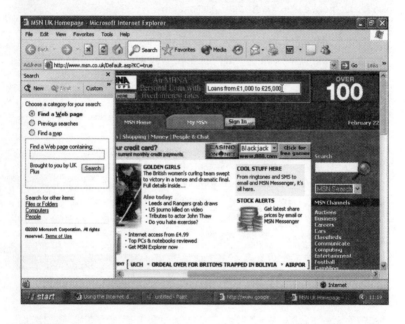

We would probably just enter our key word in the **Find a Web page containing:** slot, click the **Search** button and wait for the results. As mentioned earlier, we can greatly change the results of the search by modifying the key words entered, and this is discussed later.

There is also a lot more to searching than simply accepting the search tools presented to us by default by our browser. In fact, behind the **Search** button on your browser there may be several search programs working to find the information you request from the Internet.

Most of these **search tools** are known as **search engines**, while a few, although used in a similar way, are known as **directories**. You can see the search tools used by **MSN** by clicking **Custom** from the search window shown on the previous page.

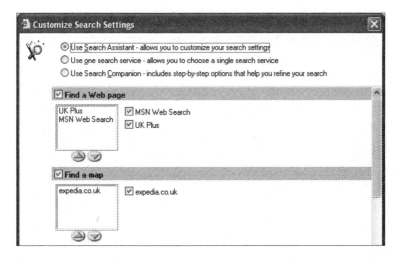

When using more than one search tool, if one doesn't find the required result, the others may - the search tools don't all work in the same way

Netscape gives a choice of search tools, namely **Espotting**, **Excite** and **UK Plus** as shown below. Also note that **Netscape** displays a list of *categories*. Selecting a category, such as **Science**, ensures that any search is already confined to the right sphere. This reduces the number of irrelevant search results compared with an unrestricted search of the entire World Wide Web.

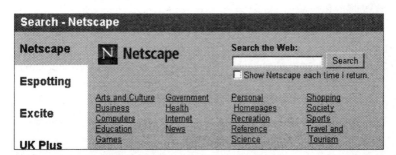

Search Engines and Directories

There are two main types of search tool, **Search Engines** and **Directories**. Although used in a similar way, they differ in the way they are created.

Search Engines

The search engine is an enormous index of millions of Web pages and their addresses. The index is created by a program known as a **robot**, **spider** or **crawler**. This visits every page and follows every link on a new Web site, then copies the text of the pages to its index, along with the address details. This process is repeated at regular intervals to keep the index up-to-date. When you request a search of the Web, the search engine returns a list of the pages which match the search criteria. Clicking on a link in an entry in the results list calls up the Web page.

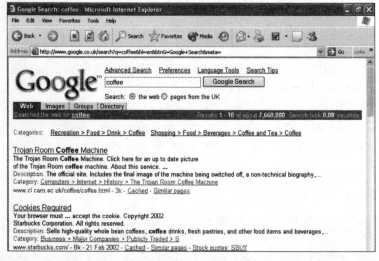

Well known search engines include Google, Excite, AltaVista, Lycos, HotBot, Ask Jeeves and Northern Light. Google is a very popular search engine which can be run from its search site at **www.google.co.uk**.

For more information and details of the vast number of alternative search engines, **www.searchenginewatch.com** is well worth a visit.

Directories

A directory is used to search for information in a similar way to a search engine. The difference is that a directory is compiled by a human, unlike the search engine index which is created by a computer. When a Web designer submits the details of their Web pages for inclusion in a directory, a short description is also provided. A human editor reviews the descriptions and then examines the Web sites. If considered suitable, the details of the Web site are included in the directory. Well known directories are Yahoo! and LookSmart.

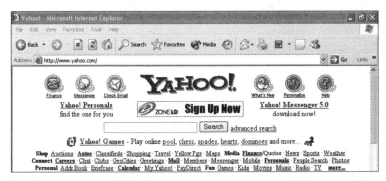

As shown above, in Yahoo!, you can enter key words in the search bar and click the **Search** button just as if you were using a search engine. However, a major difference with directories is that the information is arranged in *categories*, as shown in the following extract from the main Yahoo! screen.

With a directory you can follow down through the categories to narrow your search. You can also enter a key word or phrase and search within a category. Although searching a directory yields fewer results than a search engine, the Web pages found should be highly relevant since you have already focused on the right category.

The various search engines might at first seem to be separate entities produced by different organizations. However, there are all sorts of associations and alliances between the various companies. So that although you type your query into one particular search engine or directory, the answers may be provided by a different search tool.

At the end of a list of Yahoo! search results there are links to some of the major search engines, shown below under **Search in other search engines**. These should increase the success of the search.

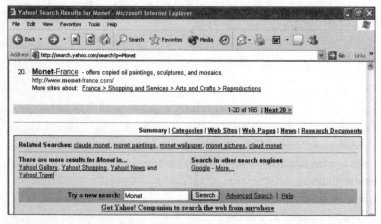

The reason for these alliances is that the search engine and directory companies make their living from the advertisements which decorate their pages. In order to attract advertising, the search engines and directories must be able to prove that they are heavily used, i.e. they receive large numbers of "hits" or visits from people browsing the Web. To increase their presence on the Web and therefore the number of hits, the companies behind the search engines and directories pay large sums to other companies willing to include links to their search engines or directories.

Searching with Google

Google is a popular search engine developed by Stanford University. It is fast and powerful yet easy to use. To start using Google, log on to the Web site at **Google.co.uk** or **Google.com**.

As shown above, you can add a **Google** toolbar to Internet Explorer. To start a search, simply type your key words in the search bar then press **Enter** or click the **Google Search** button. To go straight to the first Web page returned by **Google**, click **I'm Feeling Lucky**. Notice also that you can choose to search the entire Web or search only pages from the UK.

As mentioned earlier, the search can be greatly affected by the number of key words entered and there are various other techniques which have the effect of either narrowing down or widening the scope of a search. These are discussed shortly, but for the time being we'll look at a search for a popular "classic" car from the sixties, the Austin Mini Cooper. Although I have entered **"austin mini cooper"**, the same results will be obtained whether you use upper or lower case letters or a mixture.

When the previous search was carried out using Google, 9,060 results were returned in no time at all - the actual search took only 0.35 seconds, as shown across the top of the results list below.

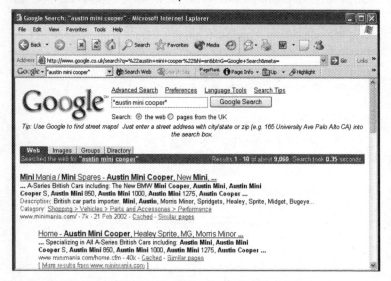

Notice that each entry starts with one line of underlined text. This is the page title; clicking in this line opens up the Web page. The text underneath the title is an extract from the actual Web page, with the key words shown bold. At various places in the results list, *categories* are listed which link to further information which may be relevant.

In the above example, **www.minimania.com/** is the URL or Web address of the first search result. When two or more pages from the same Web site are included in the results, the most relevant result is listed first, followed by the other results from the same site, shown *indented*.

7k (7kilobytes) in the first result refers to the amount of text in the corresponding Web page.

In Google, pages are ranked (i.e. placed near the top of the results list) based on several criteria. A page with many links to it from other pages is considered to be important and ranked highly.

Cached Pages

In order to compile its index, the Google search engine "crawls" a Web site and makes a copy of every page, which is stored in a "cache". Clicking the title line in a results list should lead you to the Web page. If the Web page is not accessible for any reason, you can retrieve the crawler copy from the search engine cache. Click on the word **Cached** in the relevant entry in the results list. The cached pages may not be identical to the latest Web pages but they should still be useful.

Advanced Searching with Google

There is a link to set up more precise searches on the main Google window. Click the words **Advanced Search** as shown below.

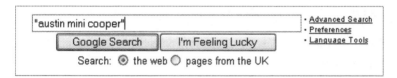

The **Advanced Web Search** window appears, allowing you to specify the way Google will match Web pages with the key words you have entered as your search criteria.

There is a choice of languages for the returned Web pages and an option to specify where your key words should appear on the page, e.g. in the title. Google can restrict a search to a particular Web site or domain, or exclude a site from the search. The **SafeSearch** filter is used to exclude sites which may be considered unsuitable for children.

The Basics of Searching

Although there are some differences between individual search engines, there is a set of basic rules of searching which generally apply. Precise details of which commands apply to which search engines can be found at **http://searchenginewatch.com/** in the feature entitled "Search Engine Features For Searchers". The following pages give an overview of some of the most common commands. When entering the key words in the search bar on your browser, there is no need to worry about upper or lower case letters. All search criteria are treated as lower case and the results are not case sensitive - in the example below, pages containing **austin mini**, **Austin Mini** or even **AUSTIN MINI** would be returned.

Using the + Sign to Include Terms

To make sure a word or term (such as a single character or single digit) is present in any results pages, precede the term with a space and the **+** sign when entering the search criteria.

+austin +mini	Search

The list of results will include all pages found with both the words **austin** and **mini** *somewhere within the page*. The two words need not be together on the page, or in the same order.

Searched the web for **austin mini**.   Results **1 - 10** of about **161,000**

If you were only interested in cars which had been prepared for racing, you could narrow down the search by adding an extra key word:

+austin +mini +racing	Search

Web pages will be listed in the results which contain all three words in any order, somewhere on the page.

Searched the web for **+austin +mini +racing**.   Results **1 - 10** of about **14,600**

Using the - Sign to Exclude Terms

In the previous example, some of the pages found will refer to the popular Austin Mini Cooper. Suppose we want to find all ordinary Austin Minis which are not the high perfomance Cooper model. This would be achieved by preceding the word **cooper** with a - sign.

+austin +mini -cooper	Search

The results of the search would exclude all Web pages containing the word **cooper** anywhere on the page.

Searched the web for **+austin +mini -cooper**   Results **1 - 10** of about **141,000**

Phrase Search Using " "

The addition of inverted commas (quotation marks or speech marks) around the search criteria means that only Web pages containing the *exact phrase*, i.e. all of the words *in the same order*, will be listed in the results.

"austin mini cooper"	Search

Searched the web for **"austin mini cooper"**   Results **1 - 10** of about **1,420**

Please note that, in this example, **"austin mini cooper"** only yields a relatively small number of search results. Entering the search criteria as **+austin +mini +cooper** yields far more results because this will find Web pages containing the three words *anywhere* on the page, not necessarily in close proximity. You can also combine search criteria as follows, to include only cars painted in British Racing Green.

"austin mini cooper" +"british racing green"	Search

With such a tight specification for the search criteria it's perhaps not surprising that only 4 (but highly relevant) results were found.

Searched the web for **"austin mini cooper" +"british racing green"**   Results **1 - 4** of **4**

Bookmarks and Favorites

When you have found a page you are interested in, either by entering its URL in the Address Bar or as a result of a search, you can save a link to the page, for future reference. This saves repeating a search later on.

In Netscape Navigator the saved links are known as *bookmarks*, while Internet Explorer uses the American word *favorites*. You can also save the *list of results of a search*, as discussed shortly.

Bookmarks in Netscape Navigator

In Netscape Navigator, with the required Web page displayed on the screen, click **Bookmarks** off the menu, as shown below.

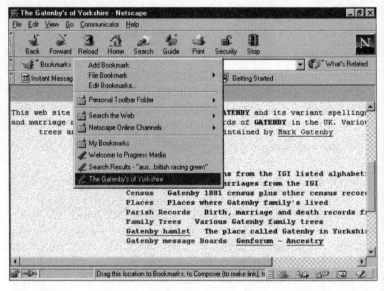

Now you select **Add Bookmark** from the menu shown above. The title of the Web page is added to the bottom of the list under **My Bookmarks**. The above menu also has an **Edit Bookmarks...** option. This allows you to delete bookmarks or organize them into folders.

Whenever you are connected to the Internet in future, any Web page which has been previously visited (and saved as a bookmark) can be accessed on-line. Simply click its entry in the list of bookmarks.

Favorites in Internet Explorer

To save a link to a Web page in Internet Explorer, select **Favorites** and
Add... off the menu. By default, the title of the Web page appears in the
Name: bar. As shown in the **Add Favorite** dialogue box below, the
default name can be replaced with a name of your choice.

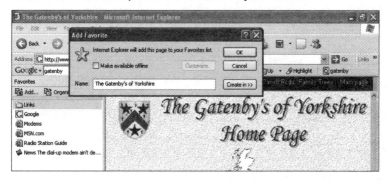

Favorites can be saved in different folders using **Create in >>** and there
is a button to create a new folder. Switching on **Make available offline**
allows you to view pages later, when not connected to the Internet.

The **Favorites** window has an option to **Organize...** favorites. This
enables entries in the favorites list to be arranged in folders and deleted
or renamed, as shown below.

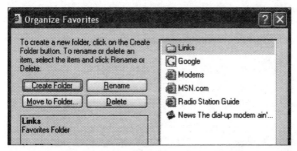

Whenever you are connected to the Internet in future, any Web page
which has been previously visited (and saved as a favorite) can be
accessed on-line (or offline if this option was switched on when the
favorite was created). Simply click its entry in the list of favorites.

Saving a Search

When a search is complete and the results are presented as a list, you can save the search site and the list of results. In Internet Explorer click **Favorites** and **Add...**. On Netscape Navigator use **Bookmarks** and **Add Bookmark**. This enables you to recall the search site and the list of search results, at some future date.

Retrieving the Results List of a Previous Search

On Internet Explorer, click on the entry for the search site in the **Favorites** panel on the left-hand side of the window shown above. This brings up the list of results from the search done at a previous time.

On Netscape Navigator, select **Bookmarks** and click **Search Results**.

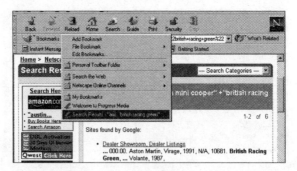

Clicking on an underlined title in the results list in the right-hand panel (shown in both screenshots above) will take you to the corresponding Web page.

The History Feature

Apart from **Favorites** in Internet Explorer and **Bookmarks** in Netscape Navigator, links to visited sites are also saved automatically. This is done by a **History** feature in both Internet Explorer and Netscape.

In Internet Explorer select **View**, **Explorer Bar** and **History** to display a list of links to recently visited sites, in a panel on the left of the Explorer window, as shown below.

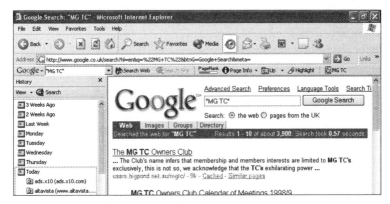

If you click one of the entries in the **History** panel, you will be connected to the corresponding Web page. You will be asked to click the **Connect** button if you are not already on-line to the Internet.

You can set the number of days for which links are kept and also clear all entries from **History**. To access these features in Internet Explorer select **Tools** and **Internet Options...** and the **General** tab.

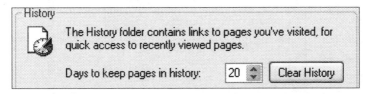

Settings for the number of days to keep pages and a **Clear History** button (shown above) are accessed from **Edit** and **Preferences....** In Netscape Navigator the **History** list appears after selecting **Communicator**, **Tools** and **History**.

Saving Information from Web Pages

Previous pages in this chapter discussed the way the *links* to Web pages can be saved using Favorites or Bookmarks. These allow you to log on to the Internet and reconnect to a Web site visited previously. It is also possible, when saving Favorites, to make a page available offline. This means the page can be viewed in Internet Explorer at a later date, without connecting to the Internet.

Copies of complete Web pages or just parts of them can also be saved on your hard disc. The information saved on your hard disc can be used in various ways. For example:

- Copy and paste the information into a word processing document, as part of a report or presentation. (While respecting any copyright issues.)

- Send a Web a page to a friend or colleague as an e-mail attachment.

- Print a copy of the information on paper to show other people, away from the computer.

Saving a Web Page to Your Hard Disc

When you are connected to the Internet, with the required page displayed on the screen in Internet Explorer, select **File** and **Save As....**

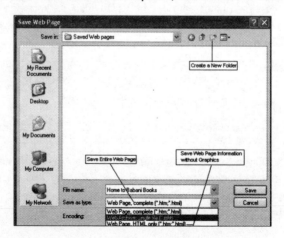

Before saving a Web page, it's often a good idea to create a new folder, using the icon shown at the top right in the **Save Web Page** dialogue box on the previous page. Then enter a name for the file and select a file format in **Save as type**:. These file types include:

Web Page, complete (*.htm, *.html)

This format saves everything on the page i.e. text, graphics files and any sound files, etc.

Web Archive, single file (*.mht)

This takes a snapshot of the Web page and saves it as a single file.

Web Page, HTML only (*.htm, *.html)

This option saves only the text, in HTML format.

Web pages saved in the above formats can be viewed off-line at a later date, in a browser such as Internet Explorer or Netscape Navigator. (The browser can be set to work off-line using the main **File** menu.)

Text File (*.txt)

This is plain text without any of the formatting features built into pages in the HTML language. A **Text File** is universally acceptable to other programs such as word processors and simple text editors like Windows Notepad and WordPad.

Netscape Navigator also uses **File** and **Save As...** to save complete Web pages for viewing off-line.

Saving Part of a Web Page

If you only want to copy say a piece of text from a Web page, a simple method (in both Internet Explorer and Netscape Navigator) is:

- Select the required text on the Web page.

- Click **Edit** and select **Copy** from the menu. This puts a copy of the piece of text onto the Windows Clipboard.

- Open the destination for the Web page extract. This might be a Microsoft Word document, for example.

- Select **Edit** and **Paste** to place the Web page extract onto the page in the document, which can now be saved.

Saving a Graphic Image from a Web page

While connected on-line to the Internet, with your browser (e.g. Internet Explorer or Netscape Navigator) displaying the required Web page:

- Right click over the image to be saved. A small menu appears as shown on the top left below, with a disc icon enabling you to save the picture in a folder of your choice. There are also options to print the picture or send it with an e-mail.

- If you select the save option, you can enter a name for the picture and choose whether to save it in the **.bmp** or **.jpeg** formats. The picture can now be opened for viewing off-line.

- If you double click the entry for the picture in the Windows Explorer it will be opened in the **Windows Picture and Fax Viewer**.

- Both **.bmp** and **.jpeg** files can also be opened in Paint, which is supplied as a free accessory to Microsoft Windows. You might also use the highly rated Paint Shop Pro image editing software to view and possibly modify an image copied from the Internet. A copy of the graphic image can easily be printed using **File** and **Print...** from the graphics program.

Printing a Web Page

Both Internet Explorer and Netscape Navigator have options to print Web pages. From the menu select **File** and **Print...**. There is also a **Print Preview...** option showing how the pages will print on paper.

Some Web pages print perfectly while you are on-line to the Internet, while others miss out important information. If you have problems printing while on-line, try some of the methods described on the previous pages for saving information from Web pages to your hard disc. For example, select all or part of a page then use **Edit** and **Copy** in the browser to place the information on the clipboard, before using **Edit** and **Paste** to put the Web information into a word processor like Microsoft Word. Then the information can be printed like any other word processing document.

Downloading Software from the Internet

It's not always essential to travel to a shop or contact a mail order company to obtain software. Although many programs are still sold on CDs in boxed packages, there's a huge amount of software available over the Internet. This is delivered to your hard disc through the telephone lines or whatever medium connects your computer to the Internet. Much of this software is known as "try before you buy"; a fully working copy is downloaded to your machine but the program only works for an evaluation period of 30 days, typically. After this time you must make a payment to continue to use the software. Many of the well-known software packages can be evaluated and purchased in this way. These include the latest versions of Web browsers like Internet Explorer and Netscape Navigator. A site containing a large number of programs for downloading is the Shareware Web site at:

http://shareware.cnet.com/

Some programs are initially free, but users may be asked to make a voluntary donation after evaluating the software. Other programs are completely free, but do not provide all of the features of a fully working and paid for copy. Essential features like printing may be missing.

For example, you may be able to download a demonstration version of a desktop publishing program. This may allow you to create a document on screen but will not allow the document to be printed on paper.

The main disadvantage of downloading software using a typical modem and telephone line is that large programs can take several hours to download, even though files are transmitted in a compressed format in order to save time. Compression is achieved using software like PKZIP and WinZip. These strip out commonly occurring words and features in a file (such as "the") and replace them with a more compact code.

WinZip is an invaluable tool for creating compressed files (known as ZIP files) for speedy transmission over the Internet, for example as e-mail attachments. It can also be used to "decompress" or *extract* the files at the receiving end. An evaluation copy of WinZip is available from:

http://www.winzip.com/

An important feature of WinZip is the ability to create *self-extracting* compressed files. This means the ZIP files can be "unzipped" from their compressed format to a fully working format, simply by double clicking on the file name after downloading the file from the Internet. Self-extracting files have the **.exe** extension after the file name.

The Download Process

The main steps in downloading software from the Internet are:

- Connect to the Web site which contains the software, locate the **Download** section and select the required software.

- If necessary, select the download location from a choice of servers around the world.

- Click the **Download** button to start transferring a copy of the program (in its compressed format) to your hard disc.

- If the downloaded program saved on your hard disc is an **.exe** file, double click the file name in Windows Explorer or My Computer to install the software on your computer. The program should now be fully operational. If the downloaded program is a ZIP file, it will need to be unzipped using a program like WinZip, before running the installation program.

Downloading a Copy of Paint Shop Pro

To download a free evaluation copy of the very popular image editing program Paint Shop Pro, log on to the Web site and select the download page. The address is **http://www.jasc.com**.

Click the download for **Paint Shop Pro 7** and then click **Save** to place a copy of the compressed file (**psp704ev.exe**) on your computer at the end of the download. The download process begins and if you are using an ordinary analogue modem (as I am), the process will take a considerable time, as shown below.

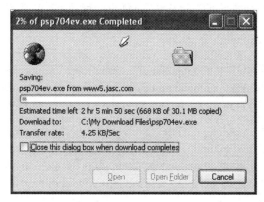

On completion of the download, a copy of the compressed file **psp704ev.exe** will be saved in your folder **C:\My Download Files** (unless you specified a different folder). Double click this file in the Windows Explorer to install a fully working version of Paint Shop Pro 7.

Summary: Using the Internet

- The Internet is a world-wide network of computers containing pages of information on virtually every conceivable subject.

- To look at various pages you need a program called a Web browser, such as Internet Explorer or Netscape Navigator.

- A collection of pages is known as a Web site, with a unique address such as **http://www.mycompany.com**. To connect to a Web site, enter the address (or URL) in the address bar of an Internet browser.

- If you don't know the address of a Web site, various *search tools* are used to look for Web pages containing key words. *Search engines* such as Google perform key word searching while *directories* like Yahoo! search Web pages in categories.

- Various simple grammatical rules enable searching to be more effective in finding Web pages containing relevant information.

- The result of a successful search is a list of Web sites matching the search criteria. Each entry in the list includes a link to a Web site and an extract from the text on the page. Clicking the link connects your computer to the Web site.

- Links to Web sites can be saved in the Favorites feature in Internet Explorer and Bookmarks in Netscape Navigator. Links to recently visited sites are automatically saved in the History feature in the main browser programs.

- Web pages can be saved on your own hard disc for future viewing and printing. Pictures can be saved separately.

- The Internet is a source of free software, including evaluation versions of major packages. The time taken to download a large program is considerable when using an ordinary modem.

Electronic Mail

Introduction

E-mail is one of the most heavily used facilities on the Internet. It has revolutionized communication between people and altered for ever the everyday routines in the office and work place. E-mail is an alternative to the conventional letter post, the fax, the telephone call and the personal visit. On the negative side, the sheer convenience of e-mail means some people are overwhelmed trying to reply to several dozen e-mails a day. Many of these are unsolicited junk mail, known as "spam". Some people miss the human contact allowed by more traditional methods of communication, such as face-to-face conversations.

The E-mail Process

Windows XP includes its own e-mail program, Outlook Express. Such a program, known as an *e-mail client*, allows you to type in new e-mails and to read and store the e-mails sent to you by other people.

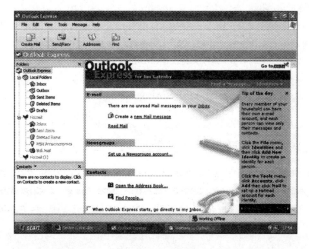

You would normally create a new e-mail message working *off-line*, after clicking **Create Mail**, as shown below on the left.

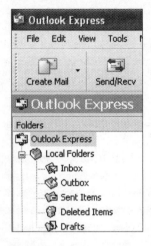

When you've entered your message, along with the e-mail address of the intended recipient, you would give the command to send the e-mail. Initially the message will be placed in the **Outbox**, shown on the left. As soon as you connect to the Internet and click **Send/Recv**, the message is sent to the mail server of your Internet Service Provider, such as MSN or AOL. A copy of your outgoing message will be kept in the **Sent Items** box on your computer, shown below on the left. Then the message is delivered and stored at the mail server of the recipient's Internet Service Provider.

Next time the recipient reads their e-mail, the new messages are downloaded to the **Inbox** on their computer and saved on their hard disc.

So when you send someone an e-mail, the message is not immediately transmitted to their computer. Although the e-mail may arrive at the recipient's ISP mail server in a matter of seconds, it will sit there unread until the recipient checks their mailbox. Of course, if you arrange to send important mail to a friend or colleague who is standing by to receive it, the whole process can be completed in a few seconds. Used in this way e-mail is much faster then conventional methods.

A major feature of e-mail is the sending of *attachments*. These are files of any sort - text, graphics, spreadsheet, sound, etc., which are "clipped" to an e-mail message and sent along with it. I have used this method to send an entire book to the printers. Large files can cause great inconvenience to the recipient because of the time to download them.

E-mail avoids the expense and inconvenience of packing and posting. Distance is irrelevant - the cost is just the charge for a local phone call.

Another major advantage of e-mail over conventional mail is the ease with which you can send multiple copies to a wide circulation list. You simply select the recipients' names from your electronic address book. If you're involved in confidential work, you can send "blind copies" so that recipients don't know who else has received a copy. There are e-mail features to automate the sending of an immediate reply to a message and to forward a copy of a message to someone else. You can arrange to be automatically notified when someone has read an e-mail that you have sent to them.

E-mails remove much of the clutter of the conventional letter post on paper, although a hard copy can be printed if necessary. E-mails can be organised efficiently into folders.

E-mail programs like Outlook Express allow the text of the message to be formatted with different fonts, graphics and in the HTML code used in Web pages. E-mails can include links to Web sites and different "stationery" or background patterns.

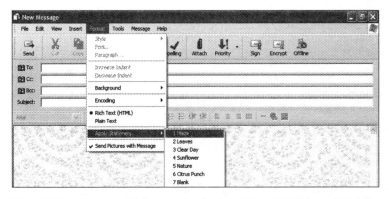

Many Web sites now include links designed to encourage visitors to contact them via e-mail. For example, someone researching their family tree may solicit responses from other family members visiting the site. When a visitor clicks a link of the type **Send us an e-mail**, their own e-mail program opens up with the reply address automatically inserted. The visitor only needs to type in the text of their message and click **Send**.

E-mail Requirements

In order to send and receive electronic mail, you need:

- An E-mail Program such as Outlook Express.
- A Connection to the Internet provided by an Internet Service Provider (ISP) or an Online Service. This will include a User Name and a Password arranged with your ISP.
- An E-mail Address arranged with your ISP.
- The names of the "mail server" computers which handle the incoming and outgoing mail at your Internet Service Provider. Examples of mail servers are:

    Incoming mail(POP3): pop3.email.msn.com

    Outgoing mail(SMTP): smtp.email.msn.com

E-mail Addresses

When you sign up for an Internet account you will be able to choose, or be given, your own e-mail address. This is a unique location enabling your mail to reach you from anywhere in the world.

Common types of e-mail address are as follows:

 stella@aol.com   james@msn.com   enquiries@wildlife.org.uk

The part of the address in front of the **@** sign is normally your *user* name or Internet *login* name. The second part of the address identifies the mail server at your company, organization or Internet Service Provider. The last part of the address is the type of organisation providing the service. In the previous addresses **.com** refers to a commercial company. Other organisation types include:

- **.edu** education
- **.gov** U.S. government
- **.org** non-profit making organisations
- **.co** UK commercial company

A two digit country code such as **uk** or **fr** may be used at the end of the e-mail address.

Setting Up Outlook Express

Before starting this work your modem or other connecting device should have a functioning dial-up connection to an Internet Service Provider (operating at local telephone rates). The ISP should have provided you with all of the necessary information including the names of their mail servers and arranged your User Name, Password and E-mail address with you.

Outlook Express is the e-mail program provided as part of Microsoft Internet Explorer, installed when Windows XP was set up on your computer. Launch the program directly from the Windows XP **start** menu or from **start**, **All Programs** and **Outlook Express**.

The first task is to create a new e-mail account, initiated by clicking **Tools**, **Accounts...**, **Mail** and **Add**. Now select **Mail...** from the small menu which pops up to start the **Internet Connection Wizard**.

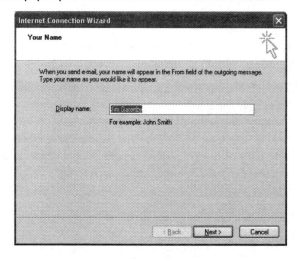

Enter your name as you would like it to be displayed on your outgoing messages, before clicking **Next** to continue.

The next dialogue box requires you to enter your e-mail address which you should have obtained from your Internet Service Provider.

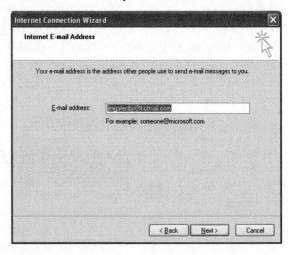

In this example I am using an e-mail address arranged with Hotmail, Microsoft's free Web-based e-mail service. After clicking **Next** you are asked for details of your mail servers, information which must usually be obtained from your **Internet Service Provider**.

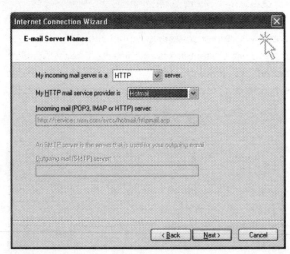

Users of Hotmail will select HTTP for this Web-based service while other users will be using either a POP3 (Post Office Protocol 3) incoming mail server or perhaps an IMAP server. POP3 servers download the mail to your computer while IMAP servers allow you to manage the mail on the server and only download the headers of each message, to save time. The next dialogue box asks for the Account **name** and **Password** which you should have arranged with your Internet Service Provider.

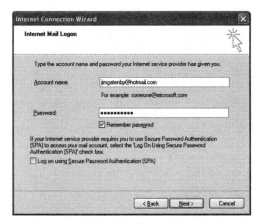

If you are concerned about unauthorized access to your e-mail then remove the tick next to **Remember password**. The final window congratulates you for successfully completing the wizard. Now click **Finish** and you are presented with the **Internet Accounts** window open at the **Mail** tab, as shown on the next page. To create additional e-mail accounts, repeat the previous procedure starting on page 255.

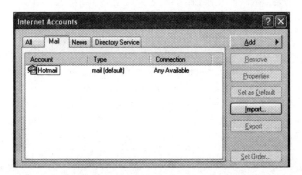

Using Outlook Express

We'll now use Outlook Express to create a simple e-mail and send it to ourselves. This may seem pointless but it's a quick way to test that the

system is working. Launch **Outlook Express** from the **start** menu then click the **Create Mail** icon on the left-hand side of the menu bar. It's basically now just a case of entering the details of the recipient(s) of your message and the

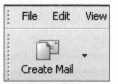

subject, before entering the message itself as shown below.

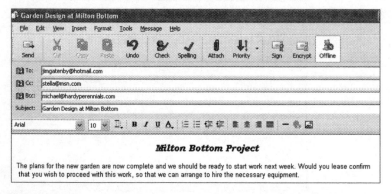

Please note that e-mail programs like Outlook Express have a useful range of text formatting effects such as different fonts, centred and justified text and also a spelling checker. There are security features such as **Sign** allowing a digital signature to be added to the e-mail, ensuring that only authorized people can read the message. **Encrypt** encodes an e-mail so that it can only be decrypted and read by certain people. The **Attach** feature allows you to send files such as Word documents along with your e-mail. Attachments are discussed later in this chapter. Please note that the e-mail message above is being entered *offline*. This is a good idea if you want to keep the telephone

line free or minimize connection charges. You can go off-line by clicking the **Offline** icon on the right-hand end of the menu bar. When offline the icon has a white background.

Creating an E-mail

Please note in the previous screenshot, showing the message creation window, there are three slots, **To:**, **Cc:** and **Bcc:**, into which recipients' e-mail addresses can be entered.

Enter the e-mail address of your main recipient in the **To:** slot. Selecting recipients for your e-mail from an electronic address book is discussed shortly.

To send "carbon" copies of the e-mail to additional recipients, list their e-mail addresses in the **Cc:** slot. In this method of sending multiple copies, everyone can see who else has received a copy of the message.

The **Bcc:** slot doesn't appear until you select **View** and **All Headers** from the Outlook Express menus. If you place e-mail addresses in the **Bcc:** slot, these "blind" recipients won't see who else has received a copy of the message.

Enter a meaningful title in the **Subject:** slot, so that the message can be easily identified at a later date. Then it's just a case of typing in your message.

Sending the E-mail

When the message is finished click the **Send** button. If you are currently working off-line you will be informed that the message will be placed in the **Outbox** until you click **Send/Recv**, as shown on the **Outlook Express Inbox** menu bar on the next page..

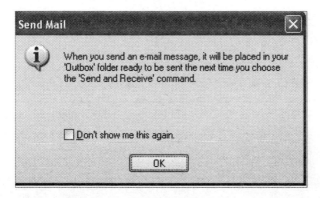

If you are working off-line and click **Send/Recv**, you will be asked if you want to go on-line.

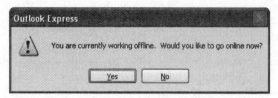

On clicking **Yes**, the dial-up connection window will appear allowing you to connect to the Internet. When you are on-line the new e-mail is sent to the mail server at your recipient's Internet Service Provider. At the same time any new mail which has been sent to you will be downloaded to your **Inbox**, as shown below.

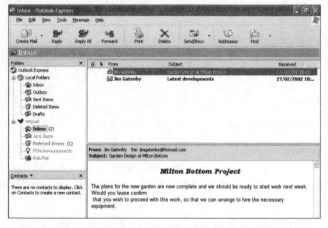

Your e-mail recipients will see your messages as soon as they log on and depending on their Internet Service Provider, their mail will probably be downloaded to the local **Inbox** on their own computer.

If you are using a Web-based Internet service like Hotmail, there is a duplicate set of Web-based folders as well as the **Local Folders** stored on your own computer's hard disc, as shown above. In Hotmail, although messages can be transferred to the local folders for archiving, they are normally kept in the Web-based folders.

Handling Incoming E-mails

Once you have read the e-mails in your **Inbox**, there are several ways of dealing with them. If the e-mail is not important you will probably want to read it then delete it by highlighting it and pressing the **Delete** key. However, this only sends them to the **Deleted Items** folder, accessed from the left-hand panel of Outlook Express when you select **View**, **Layout...** and **Outlook Bar**. To empty the **Deleted Items** folder, select **Tools**, **Options...** and **Maintenance** and make sure **Empty messages from the 'Deleted Items' folder on exit** is switched on. Then click **Apply** and **OK**. As soon as you close Outlook Express, the **Deleted Items** folder will be cleared of messages.

Saving Your E-mails

The e-mails you receive are automatically saved in your **Inbox**. However, this soon becomes cluttered and you'll probably want to store messages in folders of your own choice. From the **File** menu in Outlook Express, select **Save As...**. The **Save Message As** window appears, as shown below, allowing you to save the e-mails with a name of your choice in a folder of your choice.

There is an icon which allows you to create new folders so that you can save your e-mails in folders under different headings or categories. The saved e-mails can be viewed later by double clicking on their name in the **Windows Explorer** or **My Computer**.

Responding to E-mails

Reply

To send a reply to an e-mail sitting in your **Inbox**, select the e-mail then click the **Reply** button. (Also note **Reply All** and **Forward** below).

The Outlook Express message window opens up with the name or e-mail address of the sender of the e-mail already entered in the **To:** slot. The **Subject:** slot is automatically infilled with the original subject, preceded by the letters **Re:**.

Note that the reply also includes the text of the original message. This option can be switched off in the **Inbox** of Outlook Express after selecting **Tools**, **Options** and the **Send** tab. Then click the box next to **Include message in reply** to remove the tick, as shown below.

Reply All

Choosing this option ensures that your reply is sent to all of the recipients of the original message, whose names or e-mail addresses are automatically infilled in the **To:** slot. Otherwise **Reply All** is similar to **Reply**, with the option to include the original message with your reply.

Forward

This option allows you to send a copy of an e-mail to one or more other people. Select the message to be forwarded then enter the e-mail name or addresses in the **To:** slot. Multiple e-mail addresses should be separated by a semi-colon (;). You can also enter a short message of your own to accompany the forwarded message. The **Subject:** slot will be infilled with the original subject, preceded by the letters **Fw:**.

Using the Address Book

This feature can be used to record all of your regular e-mail contacts. Instead of typing their e-mail address every time you send them a message, you simply select their name from the list in the address book. The address book, shown below, can be opened by clicking on its icon on the top of the Outlook Express window.

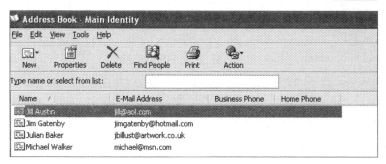

To make a new entry, click **New** as shown above and then type their details in the **Properties** window which appears.

When creating a new message, you don't need to type the e-mail addresses of contacts in your address book. Simply click the address book icon to the left of **To:**, etc., then select their names in the **Select Recipients** window shown below. Click **OK** to enter the selected e-mail addresses into the new message.

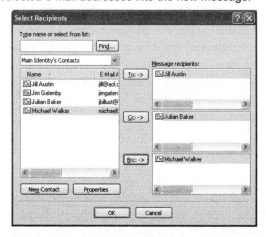

E-mail Attachments

When you send an e-mail message, you can include with it an additional file known as an *attachment*. This can be any sort of file, usually selected from your hard disc. It could, for example, be a word processing document, graphics file, or photograph.

Sending an Attachment

First the text of a new e-mail is entered in the normal way. Then click the **Attach** icon shown left or select **Insert** and **File Attachment...** from the menu bar.

The **Insert Attachment** box opens to allow you to select, from within the folders on your hard disc, the file to be attached to the e-mail. Clicking the **Attach** button inserts an **Attach:** field, an icon and file

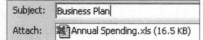

name for the attachment onto the e-mail, which is now ready to send. Now click **Send** and

the message and its attached file will be sent as a single item.

E-mailing Photographs

Photographs can be sent as attachments as described above, but they can easily occupy over 1MB, making them very slow to send and receive. However, if you right click a photograph in its folder, such as **My Pictures** in **Windows XP**, then click **Send To** and **Mail Recipient**, the **Send Pictures via E-Mail** window appears, as shown below. This allows you to make the pictures smaller and faster to send. Now select **OK** and enter the text for the message before clicking **Send**.

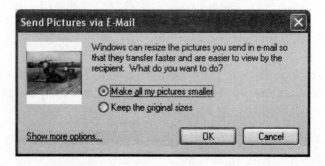

Receiving an Attachment

When the message (together with the attachment) is received into an **Inbox**, the presence of the attachment is shown by a paperclip icon. This appears on the left of the entry for the message in the **Inbox**.

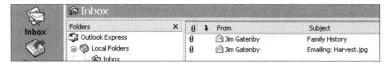

Double clicking the entry for the message in the right-hand panel of the **Inbox** opens up the message together with the attachment. If you trust the source of the e-mail, double click the entry in the **Attach:** field to view the attachment running in its own associated program. Or you can save the file to your hard disc after selecting a suitable folder.

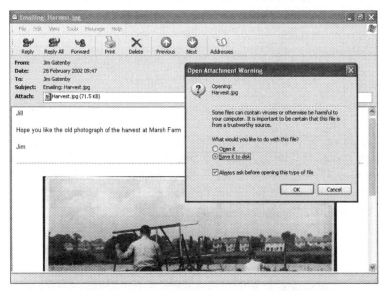

To be safe, any files you receive as e-mail attachments should be checked immediately, before opening them, using an up-to-date anti-virus program, like Norton AntiVirus or Dr. Solomon's Anti-Virus Toolkit. If you are using MSN Hotmail, incoming and outgoing attachments are checked automatically using McAfee VirusScan.

Summary: Electronic Mail

- Windows XP provides Outlook Express, a powerful and easy to use program known as an *e-mail client*.

- Before setting up an e-mail account, you must arrange a personal user name, password and e-mail address with an Internet Service Provider. You will also need details of their mail server computers and a connection to the Internet.

- Hotmail is a free e-mail service which is based on a Web site, rather than special mail server computers. This makes it accessible from any computer connected to the Internet.

- Creating a message is quite easy; you enter the e-mail addresses of the recipients, enter a subject then type the text of the message itself and click the **Send** button. Numerous text formatting effects are available, e.g. bold, italic, fonts, etc.

- E-mails can be sent to multiple recipients by typing their e-mail addresses or selecting them from an electronic address book. Additional copies may be sent to other recipients including blind copies to people who don't see who else has had a copy.

- Replies can be generated automatically to the sender and other recipients of a message and can include the text of the original message. Copies of a message can be forwarded to a new recipient. You can be notified automatically when an e-mail has been read by your intended recipient.

- E-mail can be sent with attached files such as word processing documents, spreadsheets, graphics or photographs. Very large files take a long time to transmit with a traditional modem and can cause inconvenience to the recipient. Windows XP has a feature to reduce the size of photographs to be e-mailed.

- E-mail attachment files increase the risk of viruses and all incoming and outgoing mail should be checked with an up-to-date virus checker.

Windows
Media Player

Introduction

Windows XP introduces version 8 of its popular multimedia feature, Windows Media Player. This is a powerful and versatile program and is one of the bonuses of installing Windows XP. The media player provides a stylish multimedia centre on your computer, enabling both sound and video clips to be played and managed. Windows Media Player is a screen simulation having similar controls to a physical music centre or video player.

However, the Windows XP Media Player is a far more versatile and powerful tool than the conventional music centre or video player. The Windows Media Player can connect to the Internet to download music, video and Internet Radio. You can also use the Media Player to transfer audio and video data between a range of local devices such as audio CDs, the hard disc of your computer and the small portable MP3 player. The following is a list of some of the uses of the Windows Media Player:

- Play your favourite music using **CD Audio** while working normally at the computer on a task such as word processing.

- Copy music from CDs to your hard disc for convenience and to create personalised playlists.

- Obtain details of audio albums and video clips such as artist, track name and genre by connecting to the Internet. This information is entered automatically into the **Media Library** from the Internet using the **Get Names** feature in the Media Player.

- Create your own audio CDs by copying music from your hard disc using the CD-burning software built into Windows XP.

- Download and play audio and video clips from the Internet, using the **Media Guide**.

- Organise and manage audio and video files and create playlists in the **Media Library**.

- Use the **Radio Tuner** to find and listen to radio stations of any type on the Internet across the world.

- Search all of the disc drives on the computer for any existing audio and video files. These are automatically added to the Media Library.

- Choose from a range of **Visualisations** - animated patterns which move in time with the music. An ample number of visualizations are supplied and you can download even more from the Internet.

- Change the styling of your on-screen media player using the **Skin Chooser**.

Using the Windows Media Player

The media player is part of Windows XP and can be launched from **start, All Programs** and **Windows Media Player**.

The media player can also be started by placing an audio CD in the drive, then switching on **Play Audio CD** as shown below in the **Audio CD** window which appears automatically.

The media player opens in its own window occupying the whole screen, as shown on the next page. Down the left-hand side are seven buttons used to select the main components of the media player. The buttons are **Now Playing, Media Guide, Copy from CD, Media Library, Radio Tuner, Copy to CD or Device** and **Skin Chooser**.

The Windows Media Player has the usual **Play**, **Stop**, **Forward** and **Reverse** buttons, etc. However, the centre of the **Now Playing** window shown above is occupied by a constantly changing colourful display, which moves in time with the music. This display is known as a **Visualization** and a large number of alternative visualizations are provided. You can change the visualization by scrolling through the

available list using the two arrows at the bottom left of the **Now Playing** window. Additional visualizations are available from the Internet after selecting **Tools** and **Download Visualizations**. This launches Internet Explorer.

If you wish to use the media player to provide background music while freeing the screen for other tasks on the computer, click the minimize button on the top right of the window. The media player will continue as an icon (shown right) on the Windows XP Taskbar at the bottom of the screen. Click the icon to restore the media player to its full size.

Skin Mode

The media player can also be switched between the normal **Full Mode** and the **Skin Mode** shown below. This can be achieved either by selecting **Skin Mode** from the **View** menu across the top of the media player window in **Full Mode** or by clicking the icon on the lower right of the media player. In the screenshot below the Windows Media Player is shown in Skin Mode against the Windows XP Desktop. The **Compact** skin has been selected after clicking the **Skin Chooser** button from **Full Mode** as shown on the previous page.

To return to **Full Mode** click the arrow icon at the lower right of the Windows XP Desktop as shown above. On clicking the icon, a menu appears allowing you to **Switch to full mode** or **Select a New Skin**.

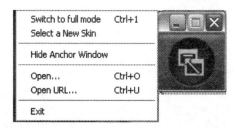

Obtaining Details of CDs

When you place a new CD in the drive, the media player starts up and plays the tracks. If you switch to the **Copy from CD** button, the window is mapped out to show all of the details of the CD. However, in the case of a new CD, many of the details may be missing such as the artist's name and the musical genre. If your computer can be connected to the Internet, you may be able to obtain this information using the **Get Names/Hide Names** button shown below.

Once the album and track information have been found on the Internet it's automatically entered into the **Media Library** - there's no need to enter any information manually.

Copying Music from CDs to Your Computer

It's very convenient to make copies of your favourite CD tracks onto your hard disc. The advantages of this include the fact that the music is always available while you are working at the computer. You don't have to search around for CDs and keep swapping them in the drive. You can also copy just a selection of your favourite tracks, so that it's possible to create personalized playlists.

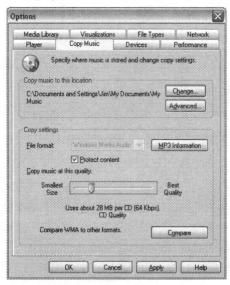

Changing Audio File Compression

Open up **Tools**, **Options...** and select **Copy Music** as shown above. You can move the slider to adjust the amount the music is compressed when recorded on the hard disc. There is a trade-off between audio quality and disc space used - the smaller the size, the lower the audio quality. An entire audio CD containing several hundred megabytes of data can be saved using only 22MB of disc space, albeit with relatively low quality. The highest audio quality requires 86MB of disc space for an entire audio CD. You can also change the destination folder on the hard disc from the default folder **My Documents\My Music** using the **Change...** button shown above.

To begin the copy process, place the required CD in the drive and select the **Copy from CD** button. By default, all of the tracks are ticked, but you can exclude tracks by clicking to remove the tick. Click the

Copy Music button to start the copying process. The **Copy Music** button changes to **Stop Copy** as shown below.

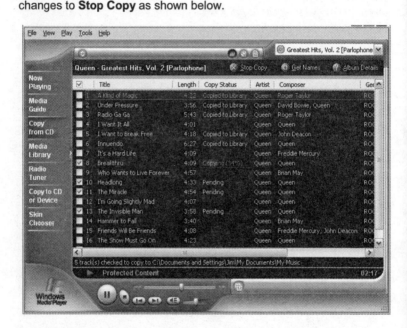

After you have copied the CD, its details are displayed in the **Media Library**, accessed via its own button on the left of the media player. The Media Library lists all of your audio and video files and allows you to compile your own playlists, using the **New playlist** and **Add to playlist** buttons.

Playing Music from CD or Hard Disc

To play music from a CD, simply insert the CD in the drive and the media player will start up automatically with the **Now Playing** feature selected. To play music which has been copied to your hard disc, start the media player and open up the **Media Library**. Select the required playlist or album and click the **Play** button to start the music.

The **Now Playing** feature gives access to a range of additional features and controls.

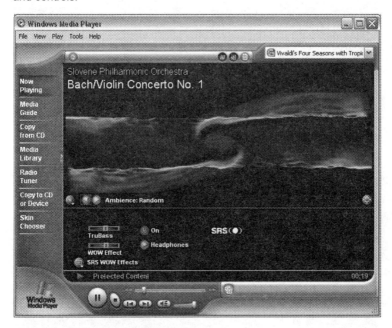

The centre of the window displays the currently selected visualization. You can cycle through the visualizations using the arrows, shown, in this example, next to **Ambience: Random**.

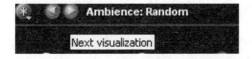

Three buttons at the top of the window allow you to display a comprehensive range of settings. The right-hand button is used to display or switch off the playlist in the **Now Playing** window. The middle button presents a choice of audio and video controls as shown below. The left-hand button *shuffles* the playlist into random order.

You can cycle through the various groups of settings, **Graphic Equaliser**, **Video Settings**, etc., using the arrows at the bottom left of the media player, just above the **Play/Pause** button.

The **Visualizations** option on the **View** menu provides an alternative way to change the visualization.

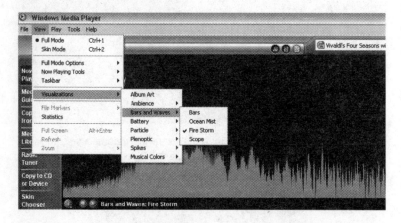

Further visualizations can be obtained from the Internet after selecting **Tools** and **Download Visualizations**.

Changing the Media Player Skin

The **Skin** is the name given to the design of the media player, its case and controls, etc., as it appears on the screen. The **Skin Chooser** button is on the left-hand side of the screen. Click the **Skin Chooser** button and you are presented with a list of skins on the left-hand side. On selecting a skin, its design appears in the right-hand panel.

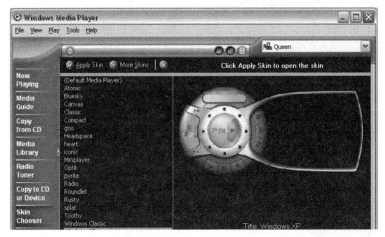

If you now click **Apply Skin**, in this example using the skin known as **Windows XP**, the Windows Media Player occupies only a small area of the Windows Desktop as shown below.

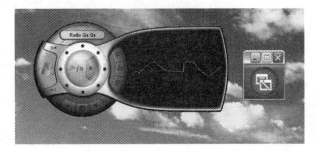

Also shown on the right of the above screenshot is the icon to return the Media Player from **Skin Mode** to **Full Mode**.

Further skins can be downloaded from the Internet after clicking the **More Skins** button. This connects you to the **WindowsMedia.com** site.

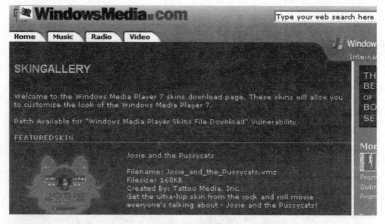

Searching Your Computer for Multimedia Files

Your hard disc(s) will almost certainly contain some audio and video files which can be played in the Windows Media Player. Perhaps you've

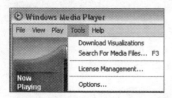

downloaded multimedia files from the Internet and aren't sure of the location. The **Search for Media Files...** option on the **Tools** menu can locate all existing audio and video files and add them to the **Media Library**. Before

starting the search, you can decide which drive(s) to search and, after clicking **Advanced**, whether you wish to include very small audio and video files. These may be part of the Windows XP operating system and not relevant to your personal Media Library.

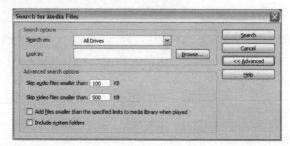

When multimedia files are found on your hard disc, entries for music files are added to the **All Audio** playlist while video files appear in the **All Clips** playlist.

In the example above, the search feature has picked up a clip from a flight simulator program. The entries in the **Media Library**, shown above in the playlist on the right of the media player, enable video clips to be selected and played. Towards the bottom left of the media player, the **Video Settings** allow you to adjust the **Brightness, Contrast, Hue** and **Saturation**. You can hide the **Video Settings** and **Playlist** by clicking on the two rightmost icons in the block of three towards the top of the media player shown left and below.

The Media Guide

Clicking this button on the media player connects you to the Internet and onto a Web page hosted by WindowsMedia.com. On this page are links to topical films, music and video.

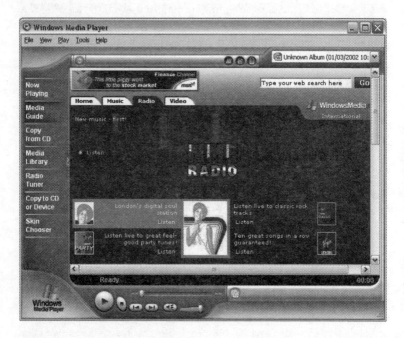

Some of these multimedia clips can be downloaded to your hard disc and played in the media player whenever required. Other pieces of music and video can be broadcast directly to your computer for immediate listening or viewing. In this process, known as "streaming", the multimedia files are not recorded on your hard disc. Currently, if you connect to the Internet via a modem, the quality of streamed video is very basic. Broadband connections, such as ADSL and cable modems, operating at least ten times faster than the traditional analogue modem, are far more suitable for streaming video.

The Radio Tuner

When you select the **Radio Tuner** button, you will be automatically connected to the Internet, assuming you have a modem and Internet connection set up and working correctly. Your media player will display a set of Internet radio stations from around the world. In addition you can search for a particular station using a range of search criteria such as keywords, the **Genre** (Oldies, Classical, Rock, etc.) the **Frequency** and the **Country**.

When you have found the radio station, while listening to the music, click **File** and **Add to Library**. This provides a link at the bottom of the **All Audio** playlist in the **Media Library**. Now highlight the entry for the radio station in the **All Audio** playlist and click the **Add to Playlist** button. A drop down menu appears from which you select the playlist in which the link to the radio station is to appear. In future, to tune in to the station, highlight its name in the playlist and click the **Play** button. If necessary, the computer will connect to the Internet and then tune in to the Internet radio station.

Downloading Music Files from the Internet

The compact size of MP3 audio files makes the format ideal for transmitting music across the Internet. Now it's possible to download music from thousands of Web sites around the world, although there have recently been legal arguments over the legality of this practice. This has led to courtroom battles between the music industry concerned about loss of revenue and those hosting the music Web sites. However, there are many sites providing copyright-free music for downloading and others where the music can be bought legally. You can find these sites by entering MP3 in your Internet search engine. One such site is **www.mp3.com,** which lists thousands of records covering all types of music.

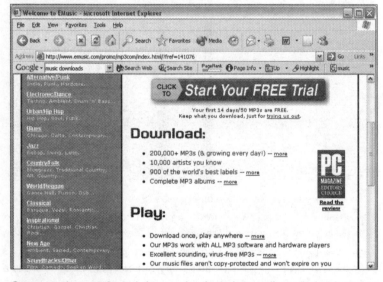

Once you have selected the music, there is usually a choice between playing the music directly across the Internet or downloading it onto your hard disc for playing later. If you have not already acquired the program RealDownload, this enhances the download process and can be obtained free from the Internet. The downloaded MP3 files are added to your Media Library from where they can be played whenever required, using Windows Media Player.

Copying Music from Your Hard Disc to a CD

Windows XP includes its own CD burning software, described earlier in this book in the context of copying of data files to CD. You can copy music to both CD-R and CD-RW media. CD-R media can only be used for one recording session, while music copied to CD-RW may not be compatible with certain types of CD player.

Copying music files from your hard disc to CD is quite simple using Windows XP and the Windows Media Player. You simply open the Media Library and highlight the album you wish to copy. Then click **Copy to CD or Device** on the media player, as shown below left.

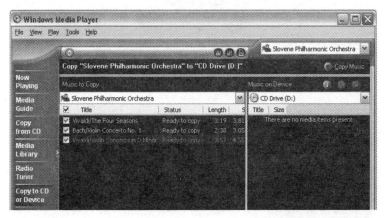

Any tracks you don't want to copy can be excluded by switching off the tick against their entry, as shown above. When you are ready, click the **Copy Music** button towards the top right of the window. Before the files are actually copied they are converted to a level of compression as specified in **Tools**, **Options...** and **Copy Music** (page 273). There is a trade off between compression and sound quality. After saving the files, they can be viewed in the Windows Explorer or My Computer. Double

clicking an icon launches the Windows Media Player and plays the track. When you put the newly created audio CD into a CD drive, Windows Media Player is launched automatically.

The Sound Recorder

If your computer is fitted with speakers and a sound card, you can record and play back sound from an external source such as a microphone or radio. **Sound Recorder** is a software component of Windows XP and is launched from the menus by selecting **start**, **All Programs**, **Accessories**, **Entertainment** and **Sound Recorder**.

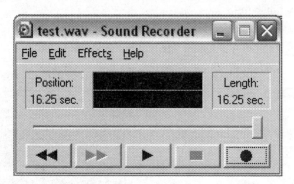

The sound recorder has the usual buttons for recording, play, stop, forward and rewind. When you've made a recording you can save it in a folder of your choice using **File** and **Save As...**. Enter a name for the file, click **OK** and it is saved with the **.wav** extension.

The sound recorder can be used to insert a sound clip in a document such as a Word file, for example. While typing the document select **Insert** and **Object...** then **Wave Sound**. You can either use the **Create New** tab to make a new recording with the sound recorder (which is launched automatically) or select **Create from File** to call up and insert an earlier sound clip saved on disc. Either way, an icon for the sound clip is placed in the document and is saved as part of the document. The sound clip can be played by double clicking the icon.

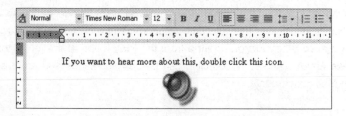

Windows Movie Maker

This component of Windows XP allows you to edit videos copied from your own camcorder. The program is launched from **start**, **All Programs**, **Accessories** and **Windows Movie Maker**. You can view a sample video provided in Windows XP by selecting **File**, **Import...**, **My Documents** and **My Videos** then selecting **Windows Movie Maker Sample File.wmv**.

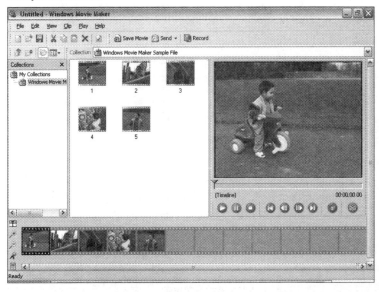

Select **Open** and a series of clips are created as shown above in the middle panel. The video is divided into clips for ease of editing. A clip can be edited by cutting or trimming and a voice-over can be added.

Each of the clips can be selected and viewed separately using the play button. The timeline along the bottom simulates a piece of film. Clips can be dragged and dropped onto the timeline to make a film in a particular sequence. Then the complete film can be played by selecting **Play Entire Storyboard/Timeline** from the **Play** menu at the top of the **Movie Maker** window. Video-clips can be sent to friends and relatives as e-mail attachments.

Summary: Windows Media Player

- Windows XP introduces Windows Media Player 8, enabling audio and video files to be played and managed.

- Audio files are played accompanied by a choice of *visualizations*. These are colourful displays which move in time with the music. CDs are catalogued in the Media Library.

- Details of albums, e.g. track title and artist, can be obtained from the Internet and automatically added to the library.

- Music CDs can be copied to a hard disc in a highly compressed format, enabling a compact and manageable music collection to be created with personalized playlists.

- When music or video is played, the Now Playing feature in the Windows Media Player enables you to cycle through and adjust a comprehensive range of audio and video controls.

- The Windows Media Player has a number of alternative designs, known as *skins*, which simulate physical media players. Additional skins can be downloaded from the Internet.

- The media player searches hard discs for any existing audio and video files and adds them to the Media Library.

- The Media Guide connects to a Web site which allows topical music and video clips to be *streamed*, i.e. broadcast directly to the PC, or downloaded and saved on the PC's hard disc.

- The Radio Tuner searches the Internet to find and connect to any type of Internet radio station, throughout the world.

- Windows Media Player includes its own CD burning software. This enables music CDs to be created by copying music files from your hard disc to a blank CD-R or CD-RW medium. Audio CDs created on CD-R are more widely compatible with CD players than audio CDs created on the CD-RW medium.

- Windows XP provides a Sound Recorder and Windows Movie Maker. These allow sound and video clips to be created, edited and saved, then played in the Windows Media Player.

Index